Scripture and Adaptive Change

How God's Word Shows Us Faithful
Transformation: A Bible Study

Nancy Meehan Yao

Parson's Porch Books

Scripture and Adaptive Change

ISBN: Softcover 978-1-960326-79-9

Copyright © 2024 by Nancy Meehan Yao

Parson's Porch Books is an imprint of Parson's Porch *&* Company (PP*&*C) in Cleveland, Tennessee. PP*&*C is a self-funded charity which earns money by publishing books of noted authors, representing all genres. Its face and voice is **David Russell Tullock** who you can contact at: dtullock@parsonsporch.com.

Parson's Porch *&* Company *turns books into bread & milk* by sharing its profits with the poor.

www.parsonsporch.com

Scripture and Adaptive Change

Dedication

I am so thankful for so many people, and for so many things. First, to my partner in marriage and ministry, Rev. James Yao, and to my family. Second, to the Presbytery of Shenandoah, which graciously allowed me the sabbatical time to work on this project. Third, to my colleagues and congregations in Shenandoah Presbyery. It is a privilege to serve the Triune God with and among you all. May we be faithful followers of Jesus, even in the midst of change.

To God alone be the Glory.

Table of Contents

An introduction to adaptive change, with descriptions of the adaptive challenges congregations are facing, and definitions of both technical and adaptive change.

Scripture: *Genesis 1:1-2:3, Luke 1: 46-55, and Matthew 15: 21-28.*

These passages illustrate foundational texts that show adaptive change, which per Heifetz et, al., is a change in "beliefs, priorities loyalties and habits."

Scripture: *Genesis 12: 1-9, Matthew 4: 18-22, Romans 12: 1-21 Genesis 19: 15-26*

Faith itself is an adaptive change. In this chapter we look at Scripture that illustrates those who make that adaptive change and follow God's adaptive challenge. We also look at one (Lot's wife) who cannot make this change and use that as a lens to ask where we as faith communities are looking backward, and whether that prevents us from faithfully following Jesus.

Scripture: *Jeremiah 29: 4-7, John 2: 1-10, Acts 6: 1-7*

Adaptive change is always context responsive, and context driven. As congregations face changes in their context of ministry, they must adapt. These passages give Biblical models of responding adaptively to changes in context.

Scripture: *Numbers 11:24-29, 2 Kings 5: 1-5, 7-15, Matthew 14: 14-16*

Adaptive change requires shifts in authority, with both a sharing of responsibility and deep listening to the voices of others. Moses models this for us, as does Jesus. In the story of the healing of Naaman, the wisdom that leads to healing comes from an unnamed enslaved girl, a reminder that we need to listen to voices that are outside our usual power structures, spheres and community.

Scripture: *Exodus 16: 1-3, Matthew 16: 13-16, 21-23, Luke 18: 18-23, Matthew 25: 14-30, Luke 8: 40-42a, Luke 8: 43-48, 49-56*

All change involves some risk and loss. We often resist change, for fear of what we will lose. These passages illustrate those who choose not to take risks, and we examine the things that might drive resistance to change. We also look at two who risk everything.

Scripture: *Luke 24: 13-17, 30-31, John 20: 19-22, and John 21: 4-7, 12-14*

In, through and after an adaptive change, there will always be elements that remain the same, and some that are entirely new and different. The post-resurrection stories illustrate this tension. We also look at examples from congregations that have made adaptive changes, look at what remains the same, and what is now different for them.

Scripture: *Acts 17: 22-32, John 3: 1-9, John 19: 38-40*

Peter, Nicodemus and Paul all illustrate the varied ways and time frames people use in making adaptive change. We also look at the church in Rome, which has been trying to operate by the technical/old standards that the Greek/Roman culture upholds, rather than the new life given to them in Christ.

Scripture: *Revelation 21: 1-4*

We are always being re-formed by God.

Prelude

I will begin with a confession…

I don't like change. I have clothes that I bought 3 decades ago, and still wear…because, well, why would I buy a new garment when I still have one that functions as a perfectly good T-shirt? I don't like it when the store rearranges the bread aisle, and I can't find the one item I went in to buy. I create a room arrangement of furniture I like and keep it that way for years.

I don't like change.

But like it or not, we know that change happens. And we know as faith communities that the world outside our doors, our ministry context, has changed…even as we have kept on doing what we've always been doing.

The PC(USA) declined in members from 1,302,043 in 2019, to 1,140,665 in 2022, a loss of 53,105 members in three years.[1] Many of us have seen similar declines in our own congregations.

The old ways of functioning as a congregation are no longer working for many of us. If nothing else, Covid-19 made this plain. But if we are honest, our ways of being church hadn't been working for some time, even before Covid. We have seen empty pews and even emptier Sunday School rooms. The old "build it and they will come" is no longer effective. More than merely numerical decline, or a temporary blip, we face a world of vast change outside our door. The decline in numbers is only a symptom. It is not simply that membership numbers are down, and thus so is giving to the church. It is not only that the church holds less sway in the world than it used to. It is that we don't know how to be a relevant body of Christ in and for the changing world.

Why, though, has the church not kept pace with change outside our doors? Urgency drives change, yet for the most part we have not felt any urgency to change, despite a multiple decades long decline.[2] There is resistance to change, for change always involves risk and loss. Change requires energy many of us simply do not have.

Seeing the need for change in business more than twenty years ago, Ronald Heifetz and others at Harvard Business School began to use the terms "adaptive change" and "adaptive challenges." Adaptive challenges are those problems which require new learning. They require tools, skills, and wisdom we do not yet have. The church is facing adaptive challenges all the time, on every front. Change is disruptive and difficult. This is true on a communal, personal, and on a neurobiological level. When we are learning new things, doing new things, we are literally re-wiring our brains. It is hard to know exactly what to do, but we are faced with the hard truth that doing what we have always been doing no longer works.

A note here about two terms used in this study: technical change/challenge, and adaptive change/challenge.

Technical change requires the use of knowledge, tools, and resources we already have or can acquire.[3] Sometimes these are called "tactical changes," which describes action that improves what is already being done in the congregation. Technical challenges require technical solutions. Got a leaky roof in the Sunday School annex? Call a roofing company. We know what to do and how to go about doing it.

I want us to note that technical solutions are not necessarily synonymous with technology but might involve technology. And that most challenges we face will require a combination of technical and adaptive responses.

Adaptive challenges require us to make changes in our "priorities, beliefs, habits and loyalties."[4] It requires that we step out in ways that are unlike "the way we've always done it," and begin to try new things. It requires flexibility and imagination and asking hard questions. Adaptive challenges are ambiguous, and in ways large or small, involve risk. They occur in an environment that is "volatile, uncertain, complex and ambiguous."[5] Adaptive challenges may make us feel uncomfortable and disoriented.

An adaptive challenge might look like this: you have a leaky roof in the Sunday School annex, which is a vastly underused space, as there have been no Sunday School classes for children/youth in at least a decade, and the adult Sunday School likes to meet in the parlor anyway, so nobody really uses that space much anymore.

We know that we are facing an adaptive challenge when it is persistent, when all the previous solutions we have tried: ignoring the leak, getting a different (and better) roofing contractor, and repeatedly throwing tarps over the roof or more money at it, do not solve the problem.

The first step in discerning that a challenge is adaptive will be to step back and begin by asking different kinds of questions. These questions will not be: who is on the Building and Grounds committee? And who is the best roofing contractor in town? They will be questions that begin: What is God calling us to do at this moment, or with this asset? Is this challenge a nudge by the Holy Spirit to do something different? Is there a need in our larger community that might make use of this space? If so, are we willing to repair the roof? Would being better stewards of the resources entrusted to us include tearing down/repurposing the Sunday School annex and creating emergency shelter for unhoused people? Or a food pantry/feeding ministry? Or a day center for the elderly?

Responses to an adaptive challenge are needed when there is no "clear-cut solution available."[6] Adaptive responses call for us to be involved with, and in communication with, other partners in the community—senior services, child-welfare programs and local schools, AA/NA groups, and to listen deeply and well to their knowledge of the talents and the needs of the community.

All this may sound daunting, even impossible.

But there is hope.

I believe that in our Scriptures, there is a narrative not only of change, but of adaptive change.

Scripture, God-breathed, shows us, again and again, adaptive change. The Living Word of God is "most alive when it is most transformational."[7]

As Presbyterians, we say in our ordination vows for Teaching Elders, Ruling Elders and Deacons that Scripture, for us, is "the unique and authoritative witness to Jesus Christ in the Church universal, and God's Word to you."[8] And in our confessions, we say that the Holy Spirit rules our faith and life in Christ through Scripture.[9] Scripture, therefore, has authority for us, certainly more (I hope) than anything that comes out of a business school, or in a flashy "5-step plan to build attendance and giving in your congregation" that you see online.

This study will be looking at Scripture passages that model adaptive change for us. We will look intentionally at aspects of adaptive change that are demonstrated in those specific narratives.

In any adaptive challenge, we will notice some things:

that adaptive change is a faithful response,

that adaptive change is context driven and context responsive.

It will require changes in authority,

and will also include risk, loss and failure (although we will also re-examine what "failure" looks like).

In and through adaptive change, there will be elements that remain the same, as well as those that are completely new and different.

Adaptive change might occur immediately or might occur over a span of time.

And we will be changed because adaptive change, as it requires, per Heifetz, changes in our loyalties, habits and preferences.

I believe that our very faith, our response to God's Good News given to us in Jesus Christ, is, itself, an adaptive change.

While all of this might be overwhelming, it is also okay. It is more than okay.

You know why? Because we worship a God who is all about doing a new thing: "See, I am about to do a new thing! Do you not perceive it?" Isaiah 43:19[10]

Our PC(USA) Book of Order reminds us that "Christ gives to the Church all the gifts necessary to be His body."[11]

The gift of adaptive change and faith filled adaptive response is a gift that Christ gives to us as the church. Scripture shows us the way.

NOTES

1. I am a pastor in the Presbyterian Church, (USA), but similar statistical trends apply to many denominations. "Comparative Summary of Statistics," Office of the General Assembly, Presbyterian Church (U.S.A.), accessed September 22, 2023, https://pcusa.org/site_media/media/uploads/oga/pdf/st atistics/2022_stats_comparativesummaries.pdf

2. John Kotter, "The 8-Step Process for Leading Change," accessed December 5, 2023, https://www.kotterinc.com/8-steps-process-for-leading-change.

3. Alan J. Roxburgh and Fred Romanik, *The Missional Leader* (San Francisco: Jossey Bass, 2006), 146.

4. Ronald A. Heifetz, Marty Linsky, and Alexander Grashow, *The Practice of Adaptive Leadership: Tools and Tactics for Changing Your Organization and the World*, 1st edition (Boston, Mass: Harvard Business Press, 2009), 19.

5. Gavin Wright and Ivy Wigmore, "What does VUCA really mean?" accessed December 5, 2023, https://www.techtarget.com/whatis/definition/VUCA-volatility-uncertainty-complexity-and-ambiguity.

6. Peter Coutts, *Choosing Change: How to Motivate Churches to Face the Future* (Herndon, VA: The Alban Institute, 2013), 77.

7. Bruce G. Epperly, *Process Theology*, (Edinburgh, Scotland: T & T Clark International, 2011), 120.

8. PC(U.S.A.) *Book of Order* 2023-2025 (Louisville, KY: The Office of the General Assembly, Presbyterian Church (U.S.A.), 2023), W-4.0404 (b),108.

9. *PC(U.S.A.) Book of Confessions*, "A Brief Statement of Faith," (Louisville, KY: Office of the General Assembly, Presbyterian Church (U.S.A.), 2016), 312.

10. Division of Christian Education of the National Council of Churches of Christ in the U.S.A, *New Revised Standard Version Bible* (San Francisco, CA: HarperOne, 2007) All Scripture used is from the NRSV, unless otherwise noted.

11. *PC(U.S.A.) Book of Order 2023-2025* (Louisville, KY: The Office of the General Assembly, Presbyterian Church (U.S.A.), 2023), F-1.0301, 2.

Chapter One

"In the beginning…"

In the beginning, God created…change.

But as Presbyterians, we have a heritage and a theology that has traditionally understood God as One who does not change. A God who acts in ways that are, and is, in God's own self, "eternal and immoveable."[1]

Even our hymns reflect this view of a God who does not change.

"Great is Thy faithfulness" we sing: "There is no shadow of turning with thee…thou changest not… as Thou has been, Thou forever wilt be…" and "naught changeth Thee."[2] More recent songs continue this depiction: Chris Tomlin's Unchanging (2002), and Cindy Berry's Almighty, Unchangeable God, written in 1969, both sing of divine immutability.[3]

The Westminster Confession, one of our foundational confessional documents, draws from a description of a God who "freely and unchangeably ordains whatsoever comes to pass," and that God is static: "without body, parts, or passions, immutable…"[4]

But Scripture shows us a God who creates change and is with us in every change.

Abram and God converse—maybe even argue—in Genesis 18, about God's choice to smite Sodom. God changes God's mind, after hearing Abram's arguments. The prophets Jeremiah and Amos also speak about God's relenting/changing God's mind.

The entire book of Jonah is based upon the premise that God can and will change God's mind and intentions for a people. In Jonah 4:2, the prophet cries to God, about God's changing God's mind about the people (and cattle) of Nineveh: "I knew that you are a gracious God and merciful, slow to anger, and abounding in steadfast love, and ready to relent from punishing."

Like Jonah, the prophet Joel also quotes Exodus 34:6, talking about a God who is not only "slow to anger, and abounding in steadfast love," but again, "relents from punishing." (Joel 3:14) That word for relenting, in Hebrew, can have connotations of regretting, of being moved with compassion, of changing one's mind.[5] Our English word, relent, is based on the Latin word *lentus*, meaning flexible.[6]

Asking God to relent and show mercy, the psalmist cries "Turn, O Lord! How long?" (Psalm 90:13) If we worshipped a God who was not flexible, but was only immoveable and static, would we even bother to pray? If we understand God as one who is only unchanging, it is no wonder we have trouble with change personally, and in our churches. Not changing might be seen as "ordained," almost holy.

I don't want us to think that the God we worship is capricious or fickle. I don't believe that is what Scripture shows us. God is "ever about the business of making new decisions for new times and places…which decisions are always in consonance with God's most basic purposes to bring salvation to all."[7]

We see in Scripture a God who is constant, and at the same time, changing and creating change. A God who is known in steadfast love and is faithful in seeking always to be in relationship with humanity and creation and is also always doing a new thing. Being a faithful church will always involve being open to, and joining in, the new thing that God is doing, in our midst, and in the world. This openness to change "reflects the ongoing divine-human call."[8]

Our divine-human interaction is always with a God who changes, who adapts to changes in context, who relates to God's people (and all creation) with imagination, flexibility and creativity.

We see this creativity at work in the first book of Scripture.

Genesis 1:1-2:3

In the beginning when God created[a] the heavens and the earth, 2 the earth was a formless void and darkness covered the face of the deep, while a wind from God[b] swept over the face of the waters. 3 Then God said, 'Let there be light'; and there was light. 4 And God saw that the light was good; and God separated the light from the darkness. 5 God called the light Day, and the darkness he called Night. And there was evening and there was morning, the first day.

6 And God said, 'Let there be a dome in the midst of the waters, and let it separate the waters from the waters.' 7 So God made the dome and separated the waters that were under the dome from the waters that were above the dome. *And it was so. 8 God called the dome Sky. And there was evening and there was morning, the second day.*

9 And God said, 'Let the waters under the sky be gathered together into one place, and let the dry land appear.' And it was so. 10 God called the dry land Earth, and the waters that were gathered together he called Seas. And God saw that it was good. 11 Then God said, 'Let the earth put forth vegetation: plants yielding seed, and fruit trees of every kind on earth that bear fruit with the seed in it.' And it was so. 12 The earth brought forth vegetation: plants yielding seed of every kind, and trees of every kind bearing fruit with the seed in it. And God saw that it was good. 13 And there was evening and there was morning, the third day.

14 And God said, 'Let there be lights in the dome of the sky to separate the day from the night; and let them be for signs and for seasons and for days and years, 15 and let them be lights in the dome of the sky to give light upon the earth.' And it was so. 16 God made the two great lights—the greater light to rule the day and the lesser light to rule the night—and the stars. 17 God set them in the dome of the sky to give light upon the earth, 18 to rule over the day and over the night, and to separate the light from the darkness. And God saw that it was good. 19 And there was evening and there was morning, the fourth day.

20 And God said, 'Let the waters bring forth swarms of living creatures, and let birds fly above the earth across the dome of the sky.' 21 So God created the great sea monsters and every living creature that moves, of every kind, with which the waters swarm, and every winged bird of every kind. And God saw that it was good. 22 God blessed them, saying, 'Be fruitful and multiply and fill the waters in the seas, and let birds multiply on the earth.' 23 And there was evening and there was morning, the fifth day.

24 And God said, 'Let the earth bring forth living creatures of every kind: cattle and creeping things and wild animals of the earth of every kind.' And it was so. 25 God made the wild animals of the earth of every kind, and the cattle of every kind, and everything that creeps upon the ground of every kind. And God saw that it was good.

26 Then God said, 'Let us make humankind[c] in our image, according to our likeness; and let them have dominion over the fish of the sea, and over the birds of the air, and over the cattle, and over all the wild animals of the earth,[d] and over every creeping thing that creeps upon the earth.'

27 So God created humankind[e] in his image,
in the image of God he created them;[f]
male and female he created them.

28 God blessed them, and God said to them, 'Be fruitful and multiply, and fill the earth and subdue it; and have dominion over the fish of the sea and over the birds of the air and over every living thing that moves upon the earth.' 29 God said, 'See, I have given you every plant yielding seed that is upon the face of all the earth, and every tree with seed in its fruit; you shall have them for food. 30 And to every beast of the earth, and to every bird of the air, and to everything that creeps on the earth, everything that has the breath of life, I have given every green plant for food.' And it was so. 31 God saw everything that he had made, and indeed, it was very good. And there was evening and there was morning, the sixth day.

2:1 Thus the heavens and the earth were finished, and all their multitude. 2 And on the seventh day God finished the work that he had done, and he rested on the seventh day from all the work that he had done. 3 So God blessed the seventh day and hallowed it, because on it God rested from all the work that he had done in creation.

Many of us grew up hearing Genesis 1 in the King James version: "In the beginning, God created…", but the Hebrew of this text supports a reading of: "In the beginning of God creating…" or even "when God began creating," which gives an ongoing, dynamically changing effect to this Scripture.[9]

23

And God's first action is one of change. Where there was only "void and vacuum," God says… "Light. And there was light."[10]

The first action, the first word of God, in the very first book of our Scripture…is one of change. The entire creation narrative is one of imaginative, creative change! God continues to act in new, creative ways.

Luke 1:46-55

[46] *And Mary[a] said,*

'My soul magnifies the Lord,
[47] and my spirit rejoices in God my Saviour,
[48] for he has looked with favour on the lowliness of his servant.
*   Surely, from now on all generations will call me blessed;*
[49] for the Mighty One has done great things for me,
*   and holy is his name.*
[50] His mercy is for those who fear him
*   from generation to generation.*
[51] He has shown strength with his arm;
*   he has scattered the proud in the thoughts of their hearts.*
[52] He has brought down the powerful from their thrones,
*   and lifted up the lowly;*
[53] he has filled the hungry with good things,
*   and sent the rich away empty.*
[54] He has helped his servant Israel,
*   in remembrance of his mercy,*
[55] according to the promise he made to our ancestors,
*   to Abraham and to his descendants for ever.'*

We know this passage as "the Magnificat," in which Mary says, "my soul magnifies the Lord." Mary says/sings this after the astounding angelic

24

announcement that she is pregnant with a child by the Holy Spirit—which, I imagine, was an unexpected and perplexing change in her life. If ever there is an adaptive change ranking, this encounter will be near the top of that list.

Mary, though, continues: "My spirit rejoices in God my Savior," even in the midst of this huge, life altering, maybe even life-threatening change. And the song she sings/pronounces is one of God making HUGE change. The powerful will be thrown down from their places of power, the hungry filled with good things to eat, and the rich sent away empty. God is making change, overturning injustice in the world. For Mary, and for us, the change is Jesus, and all the systems of the world, and divisions of humanity, will be changed.

We see adaptive change in Jesus' own life, as well.

Matthew 15:21-28

²¹ Jesus left that place and went away to the district of Tyre and Sidon. ²² Just then a Canaanite woman from that region came out and started shouting, 'Have mercy on me, Lord, Son of David; my daughter is tormented by a demon.' ²³ But he did not answer her at all. And his disciples came and urged him, saying, 'Send her away, for she keeps shouting after us.' ²⁴ He answered, 'I was sent only to the lost sheep of the house of Israel.' ²⁵ But she came and knelt before him, saying, 'Lord, help me.' ²⁶ He answered, 'It is not fair to take the children's food and throw it to the dogs.' ²⁷ She said, 'Yes, Lord, yet even the dogs eat the crumbs that fall from their masters' table.' ²⁸ Then Jesus answered her, 'Woman, great is your faith!

Let it be done for you as you wish.' And her daughter was healed instantly.

This is the story of the Canaanite woman and Jesus, or, as I like to call this story "A woman talks back to Jesus," or even, #neverthelessshepersisted.

Jesus is very clear and firm in his words and intent in this interaction. An indigenous woman, a Canaanite, (not of Hebrew descent) sees Jesus, and begs him to help her daughter.

At first, Jesus doesn't even bother to answer her. Not only that, but Jesus also then explicitly states that he is only for "the lost sheep of Israel." (15:24). A Canaanite woman would definitely not be counted as one of those sheep.

Yet the woman persists, kneeling before Jesus, and arguing with him.

Jesus, upon hearing her pleas and her arguments, recognizes and praises her great faith, and the woman's daughter is instantly healed.

Writing about change, John Kotter says that all change happens in this sequence: we see a problem, we feel something, and then we change, or make change in our environment.[11] We have multiple stories about Jesus being moved with compassion, or pity. I believe that is what happened in this Scripture. This is an adaptive change, not a technical one. Remember that one of the definitions of adaptive change is a change in "priorities, beliefs, habits or loyalties." In this interaction, Jesus has certainly changed his loyalties, and shows in his actions that he now understands himself as not only for a restricted few, but for all.

So. Jesus changes his mind.

As one dear 80+ year old participant in a Bible Study, after reading the story of Jesus and the Canaanite woman and being asked what effect reading this Scripture through an adaptive change lens had for her, said, after a thoughtful pause: "well, if Jesus can change, I guess we can, too." Amen and amen.

Questions for Discussion:

Think about all the ways you have heard God described.

If you were to list the characteristics of God, would you say God was unchanging? Changing? Or something else?

Did the stories in this chapter surprise you? In what ways?

How do these Scriptures influence your thinking about adaptive change? (Do they?)

What would it look like for your church to see change as "holy," as following Jesus' example? How would that affect decisions? Do you think it makes thinking about change easier if we see it in Scripture?

Think about your congregation—how open to change are they? What would help them make necessary changes?

NOTES

1. *PC(U.S.A.) Book of Confessions*, "The Larger Catechism," 7.122, 196.

2.Thomas Chisholm. "Great is Thy Faithfulness." (Carol Stream, IL: Hope Publishing Company), 1923, 1951, Walter Chalmers Smith, text, "Immortal Invisible, God Only Wise," 1867.

3.David T. Lamb, "The Immutability of YHWH," *Southern Theological Review*, 2/1 (Summer 2011): 25.

4. *PC(U.S.A.) Book of Confessions*, "The Westminster Confession of Faith," 6.011, 6.014, 151-152.

5. Lamb, 30.

6. Lamb, 31.

7.Terence E. Fretheim, "The Repentance of God," in *What Kind of God? Collected Essays of Terence E. Fretheim*, Michael Chan and Brent Strawn, ed. (University Park, PA: Penn State University Press, 2015).

8. Catherine Keller, *On the Mystery* (Minneapolis, MN: Fortress Press, 2008), 128.

9. William P. Brown, *The Seven Pillars of Creation* (New York, NY: Oxford University Press, Inc., 2010), 252.

10. Ibid., 253.

11. John P. Kotter, *The Heart of Change* (Boston, MA: Harvard Business Review Press, 2002), 179.

Chapter Two

Follow Me....

If we define adaptive responses as ones that require a change in belief, habits, loyalties and priorities, (and we do), then a life of faith itself is one ongoing journey of adaptive response to God's gracious action and call.

Sometimes that life of change, that turning and following, might not seem to make much sense. Adaptive challenges often arise when the way is not clear, and adaptive responses often don't match our (or others) ideas about what an appropriate solution looks like, or even "what works."

Genesis 12:1-9 - The Call of Abram

12 Now the LORD said to Abram, 'Go from your country and your kindred and your father's house to the land that I will show you. ² I will make of you a great nation, and I will bless you, and make your name great, so that you will be a blessing. ³ I will bless those who bless you, and the one who curses you I will curse; and in you all the families of the earth shall be blessed.'[a]

4 So Abram went, as the LORD had told him; and Lot went with him. Abram was seventy-five years old when he departed from Haran. ⁵ Abram took his wife Sarai and his brother's son Lot, and all the possessions that they had gathered, and the persons whom they had acquired in Haran; and they set forth to go to the land of Canaan. When they had come to the land of Canaan, ⁶ Abram passed through the land to the place at Shechem, to the oak[b] of Moreh. At that time the Canaanites were in the land. ⁷ Then the LORD appeared to Abram, and said, 'To your offspring[c] I will give this land.' So he built there an altar to the LORD, *who had appeared to him.* ⁸ *From there he moved on to the hill country on the east of Bethel, and pitched his tent, with Bethel on the west and Ai on the east; and there he built an altar to the* LORD *and invoked the name of the* LORD. ⁹ *And Abram journeyed on by stages towards the Negeb.*

I have often wondered about the conversations not recorded in our Bibles, including between Abram and Sarai.

Abram receives this call from God...and what? Goes home and says to Sarai "guess what! We are going...to somewhere that I don't know yet...just pack the camels. We will leave in the morning."

Verse 4 says "so Abram went..." without any backstory or hint of what was said...or not said. Perhaps there was a lot of uncomfortable silence on this trip!

Abram doesn't know where this journey will take him. Yet he trusts in God.

We see Abram's adaptive response: he leaves his family and home, and, some commentators say, his original faith community. He changes his priorities, habits, and loyalties...all to follow God's instruction. Abram turns from what he has known into the unknown.

We say that we "turn from sin and turn to Jesus Christ our Lord and Savior," in our baptismal vows and the vows we make as we join a church. In the early church, those being baptized would literally turn from facing

31

west to east, physically orienting themselves to this new life in Christ.[1]

The very words for this turning, in the Bible are *shub* (Hebrew) and *metanoia* (Greek). Both words are commonly translated as "repent." And while they can and do mean that, I want to expand our definitions a bit.

"*Shuv*" can mean to turn back to God (Hosea 6:1).[2] But I want us to consider that this is not merely turning back and doing the same old things, which would be a technical response. Rather, we are turning to God with a transformed view of both God and ourselves.

"*Metanoia*," in Biblical Greek, speaks to that transformed view. It means, literally, to think differently, to have a different perspective.[3]

And while the word "metanoia" does not appear in the story of the fishermen standing on the lakeside in Galilee, we do see it in their response.

Matthew 4:18-22 - Jesus Calls the First Disciples

[18] As he walked by the Sea of Galilee, he saw two brothers, Simon, who is called Peter, and Andrew his brother, casting a net into the lake—for they were fishermen. [19] And he said to them, 'Follow me, and I will make you fish for people.' [20] Immediately they left their nets and followed him. [21] As he went from there, he saw two other brothers, James son of Zebedee and his brother John, in the boat with their father Zebedee, mending their nets, and he called

them. [22] *Immediately they left the boat and their father, and followed him.*

Note that the brothers, Simon and Andrew, upon hearing Jesus' words, immediately left their nets. The word translated as "left" has a meaning of to drop or let die.

They have a new, different perspective. They will not need those nets or boats in this new life.

In the Gospel of Luke, we see a similar or the same story, told in a slightly more fleshed out way.

Luke 5:4-11.

When he had finished speaking, he said to Simon, 'Put out into the deep water and let down your nets for a catch.' [5] *Simon answered, 'Master, we have worked all night long but have caught nothing. Yet if you say so, I will let down the nets.'* [6] *When they had done this, they caught so many fish that their nets were beginning to break.* [7] *So they signalled to their partners in the other boat to come and help them. And they came and filled both boats, so that they began to sink.* [8] *But when Simon Peter saw it, he fell down at Jesus' knees, saying, 'Go away from me, Lord, for I am a sinful man!'* [9] *For he and all who were with him were amazed at the catch of fish that they had taken;* [10] *and so also were James and John, sons of Zebedee, who were partners with Simon. Then Jesus said to Simon, 'Do not be afraid; from now on you will be catching people.'* [11] *When they had brought their boats to shore, they left everything and followed him.*

Here in Luke, the disciples also leave everything, and the same word is used. The King James Version translates it as "they forsook everything." We will see more about risk and loss in adaptive change in a later chapter but think about the risk they are taking. Think about the loss to them, and to their families.

They turn, literally and immediately, from one thing to another.

Jesus also tells the fishermen: "From now on, you will be fishing for people." While they already know how to fish for fish, some new learning will be needed. Adaptive responses always require new learning. In fact, the Biblical Greek word for disciple, "*mathetais*" means "learner or student."[4]   A life of faith is a life of learning.

But not, necessarily, learning more content. Remember the illustration of the leaky roof in the Sunday School annex? Learning more content would be finding more and/or better roofers, or perhaps learning how to repair the roof ourselves.

Adaptive challenges require us to learn to think in ways that are transformative.

Transformation often begins with a disorienting dilemma, and then prompts us to go further. It means that, among other things, we need to examine not just the problem at hand, but also our assumptions and the narratives that we both tell ourselves and live in, as individuals and communities.[5] Narratives that might include "we need the Sunday School annex, because we have always had one, because that's what churches have and do."

Reexamining our narratives can happen at any time. Recent research shows that the brain continues in "plasticity," the ability to change, even into later ages.[6] This means that we can continue to learn throughout our span of life. Again, this is not more or better content. In this growth mindset, (as opposed to a "fixed" mindset), as author Carol Dweck has said, qualities like openness, creativity, and imagination, "can be cultivated [which] leads to a host of different thoughts and actions, taking you down an entirely different road.[7]

For us, this will include learning new ways of being the church. Scott Cormode uses the term of shifting our "mental models" of what church should be like, a way of setting up categories in order to make sense of the world.[8] John Cleghorn, writing about the adaptive challenges facing Caldwell Presbyterian Church (and others), says: "the promise of the church is the transformation of its disciples as they experience healing, embrace, redemption and a renewed sense of call."[9]

Paul's letters to the early churches show us that to apply technical solutions did not work in the challenges facing new faith communities. Adaptive responses were called for, ones that would help them become the church Paul knows they are called to be.

Read Romans 12:1-21

I appeal to you therefore, brothers and sisters,[a] by the mercies of God, to present your bodies as a living sacrifice, holy and acceptable to God, which is your spiritual[b] worship. [2] Do not be conformed to this world,[c] but be transformed by the renewing of your minds, so that you may discern what is the will of God—what is good and acceptable and perfect.[d]

³ For by the grace given to me I say to everyone among you not to think of yourself more highly than you ought to think, but to think with sober judgement, each according to the measure of faith that God has assigned. ⁴ For as in one body we have many members, and not all the members have the same function, ⁵ so we, who are many, are one body in Christ, and individually we are members one of another. ⁶ We have gifts that differ according to the grace given to us: prophecy, in proportion to faith; ⁷ ministry, in ministering; the teacher, in teaching; ⁸ the exhorter, in exhortation; the giver, in generosity; the leader, in diligence; the compassionate, in cheerfulness.

⁹ Let love be genuine; hate what is evil, hold fast to what is good; ¹⁰ love one another with mutual affection; outdo one another in showing honour. ¹¹ Do not lag in zeal, be ardent in spirit, serve the Lord.[e] ¹² Rejoice in hope, be patient in suffering, persevere in prayer. ¹³ Contribute to the needs of the saints; extend hospitality to strangers.

¹⁴ Bless those who persecute you; bless and do not curse them. ¹⁵ Rejoice with those who rejoice, weep with those who weep. ¹⁶ Live in harmony with one another; do not be haughty, but associate with the lowly;[f] do not claim to be wiser than you are. ¹⁷ Do not repay anyone evil for evil, but take thought for what is noble in the sight of all. ¹⁸ If it is possible, so far as it depends on you, live peaceably with all. ¹⁹ Beloved, never avenge yourselves, but leave room for the wrath of God;[g] for it is written, 'Vengeance is mine, I will repay, says the Lord.' ²⁰ No, 'if your enemies are hungry, feed them; if they are thirsty, give them something to drink; for by doing this you will

heap burning coals on their heads.' [21] *Do not be overcome by evil, but overcome evil with good.*

In writing to the church gathered in Rome, Paul tells them that they must be "transformed by the renewing of their minds." (Romans 12: 2)

Paul is not talking about learning new or more content; rather, it is a whole transformation. They are now new people, and so old rules and habits no longer apply. They are not to be conformed. The word for conformed is *syschemetizo*, from which we get our word schematics, for a plan or model. That is, they are not to live in the same or previous patterns but are to live according to what has been revealed in Jesus Christ.[10] Newness of life requires new thinking and new (or different) kinds of relationships.

The word for transformation, *metamorphos* is a passive imperative. That is, Paul is commanding the church to *let themselves be changed* by the Spirit of God.

And Paul goes on to describe what this adaptive, transformed thinking produces.

Note how much of Paul's instruction is focused on behavior toward others: "love one another, outdo one another in showing honor...contribute to the needs of the saints, extend hospitality to strangers." This "ethos of parity" and love is in sharp contrast to the members' experience in the larger Greco-Roman society.[11] The old ways of personal, political, and corporate relations, of power over others, no longer apply in their new life as followers of Christ.

Learning new ways of being is transformative.

And learning new things is tiring.

It is much easier, from a neurobiological perspective, to keep on doing what we already know how to do. Think about driving your car. Once you learned how, and became comfortable driving, you didn't have to think so hard and in such minute detail, about how to drive, where to turn, what to pay attention to. In fact, I imagine you drive home from church without really thinking about it. The pathways in your brain are already laid down.

Learning new things, in an adaptive challenge, takes more energy. Literally: your brain uses more glucose when learning new things.[12]

It will probably feel uncomfortable. If you have ever had your dominant hand in a sling or a cast, you know how difficult it is to learn to do the most basic things: eating, writing, combing your hair, with your other hand. And while we experience this discomfort, the new learning is actually rewiring our brains, as new neural pathways are being made.[13]

But in an adaptive challenge, this feeling of discomfort, or disequilibrium, can be an opening, a prompt, a kick in the butt, to try new, adaptive ways. Heifetz talks about the "productive zone of disequilibrium."[14] Uncomfortable, perhaps, unfamiliar surely, but also productive.

Remember that "growth mindset" mentioned earlier? Many of us lived through this in the spring and summer of 2020, as the ways in which we could safely gather as congregations changed. Many of our congregations responded adaptively. We transformed the ways we worshipped, gathered together, and acted as a congregation. But it did mean a shift in our mental models of how, when and where we could be a congregation, and it did take extra energy and flexibility.

And to be honest, there are times when we choose not to respond adaptively.

Genesis 19:15-26

[15] *When morning dawned, the angels urged Lot, saying, 'Get up, take your wife and your two daughters who are here, or else you will be consumed in the punishment of the city.'* [16] *But he lingered; so the men seized him and his wife and his two daughters by the hand, the LORD being merciful to him, and they brought him out and left him outside the city.* [17] *When they had brought them outside, they[a] said, 'Flee for your life; do not look back or stop anywhere in the Plain; flee to the hills, or else you will be consumed.'* [18] *And Lot said to them, 'Oh, no, my lords;* [19] *your servant has found favour with you, and you have shown me great kindness in saving my life; but I cannot flee to the hills, for fear the disaster will overtake me and I die.* [20] *Look, that city is near enough to flee to, and it is a little one. Let me escape there—is it not a little one?—and my life will be saved!'* [21] *He said to him, 'Very well, I grant you this favour too, and will not overthrow the city of which you have spoken.* [22] *Hurry, escape there, for I can do nothing until you*

arrive there.' Therefore the city was called Zoar.[b] *²³ The sun had risen on the earth when Lot came to Zoar.*

²⁴ Then the LORD *rained on Sodom and Gomorrah sulphur and fire from the* LORD *out of heaven; ²⁵ and he overthrew those cities, and all the Plain, and all the inhabitants of the cities, and what grew on the ground. ²⁶ But Lot's wife, behind him, looked back, and she became a pillar of salt.*

Lot has been told to flee the city and is only able to summon a partially adaptive response. He leaves, but negotiates fleeing to a nearby city, Zoar, rather than following God's instructions to flee to the hills.

Lot's wife, along with her whole family, has been told not to look back. But she does, and is turned into a pillar of salt. We can have sympathy for her impulse. She has been told to leave everything she knows. But her turning back is in many ways a technical response. She resists (refuses?) letting go of the past.

I think that is often our response as churches. We look to our past, as individuals, and as congregations, even though our context of ministry has changed dramatically.

Many churches have a history room, or a history wall. It is often the first thing a visitor sees when entering a church. And while our histories have shaped us, and we are thankful for the heritage of faithful saints, if all that we are is only who we used to be, if we only do the same things the way we have always done them, then we will have chosen traditionalism over new life. Theologian Jaroslav Pelikan describes traditionalism as the dead faith of the living, as opposed to tradition, which is the living faith of the dead.[15] Churches have become "entrenched in traditionalism," because it is easier to continue in "habits and unexamined customs...rather than engaging in fruitful ministry."[16]

Our former core practices and competencies, which served us well in former times, have become, in our resistance to change, our core rigidities.[17] What previously worked has become concretized, restrictive, unyielding and unable to respond to God's call.

We will become pillars of salt, like Lot's wife.

Questions for Discussion:

How do you experience change: as delightful, as difficult or threatening, or as something in-between?

Is there a difference between choosing change, and having change thrust upon you? What changes, chosen or not, have you experienced in your life?

How has your congregation changed through the years? How much emphasis is put on the past? How flexible is your church?
Think about Paul's letter to the church in Rome. What have they been doing? And what is Paul's concern for them?

Does it make a difference in our understanding if we view this as Paul's call to change from technical solutions (the old ways of living) to adaptive change (in which the church is called to a new way of being a community)?

Action item:

For just this Sunday, sit in a place in worship other than your usual seat. While you are there, pay attention: what new things do you notice from this new spot? Which things are better? Which things are not? Later, notice how you felt, and what you have learned from this exercise.

NOTES

1. Tom Long, "Go Tell," *Follow Me Adult Reflection Guide* (Louisville, KY: Growing Faith Resources, 2022), 46.

2.Francis Brown et al., *The Brown-Driver-Briggs Hebrew and English Lexicon* (Peabody, MA: Hendrickson Publishers, Inc., 2005), 996.

3.Walter Bauer et al., *A Greek-English Lexicon of the New Testament*, 2nd edition (Chicago, IL: University of Chicago Press, 1979), 511.

4.Ibid., 485.

5.Jack Mezirow and Associates, *Learning as Transformation* (San Francisco, CA: Jossey-Bass, Inc., 2000), 34.

6. John Medina, *brain rules,* (Seattle, WA: Pear Press, 2008), 271.

7.Carol Dweck, *Mindset* (New York, NY: Ballentine Books, 2016), 6.

8. Scott Cormode, *The Innovative Church*, (Grand Rapids, MI: Baker Academic, 2020), 21.

9. John Cleghorn, *Resurrecting Church,* (Minneapolis, MN: Fortress Press, 2021), 179.

10.Amy-Jill Levine and Marc Zvi Brettler, ed., *The Jewish Annotated New Testament* (London, England: Oxford University Press, 2011), 279.

11.Charles B. Cousar, *The Letters of Paul* (Nashville, TN: Abingdon Press, 1996), 142.

12.Christopher W. Kuzawa et. al., "Metabolic costs and evolutionary implications of human brain development," *Proceedings of the National Academy of Sciences* (111 (36)): 13010-13015, accessed October 31, 2023, https://www.pnas.org/doi/10.1073/pnas.1323099111.

13.Sue Langley, "Why do people find it so hard to change when they know it's good for them?," accessed December 5, 2023, https://langleygroup.com.au/why-do-people-find-it-so-hard-to-change-when-they-know-its-good-for-them/.

14.Ronald A. Heifetz, Marty Linsky, and Alexander Grashow, *The Practice of Adaptive Leadership: Tools and Tactics for Changing Your Organization and the World*, 1st ed. (Boston, Mass: Harvard Business Press, 2009), 30.

15.Jaroslav Pelikan, The *Vindication of Tradition* (Yale University Press, New Haven: CT, 1986), 65.

16. Lisa R. Withrow, "Change: Exploring Its Implications for Religious Leadership," *Journal of the Academy of Religious Leadership*, 7, no. 2 (Fall 2008): 48, accessed December 22, 2020, http://arl-jrl.org/wp-content/uploads/2016/02/Withrow-Change-Exploring-its-Implications2008-Fall.pdf

17.Robert Stephen Reid, "Becoming a Built to Change Congregation," *Journal of Religious Leadership* 13, no. 1 (Spring 2014): 32, accessed October 24,2023, http://arljrl.org/wp-content/uploads/2016/02/Reid-Becoming-a-Built-to-Change-Congregation-2014.pdf.

Chapter Three

Context is everything…and context is changing

Bill Gates has said "content is king." Gary Vaynerchuk, another entrepreneur, expanded that, saying "if content is king, then context is God."[1]

Now, I am in no way saying that context is the God we know and worship, but I believe that God is found in every context, and that in a changing context, we need to specifically and faithfully ask: "Where is God in this? And how can we join in the grace and mercy and new thing God is doing?"

We know the context of our ministry has changed and continues to change.

And while all this change might seem sudden, I want you to think about the history of your congregation. (I know, I talked about getting "stuck" in our histories in the previous chapter…but bear with me for a minute.)

Many of us worship in congregations that were established generations ago. In Shenandoah Presbytery where I serve, there are churches dating back to prior to the Revolutionary War. Many others of us worship in congregations that were established in the mid-19th or early 20th century.

But I imagine no one reading this today came to church in a mule-pulled wagon, or worshipped by lantern light, or had no running water or bathroom facilities available to them while at church.

We have a fixed idea of "how church is supposed to be." This is based on our own experience and memories, or perhaps the experience of the previous generation.

In the more recent past, meaning post-World War II, going to church was simply what most people did on Sunday morning. It was a given, seen not only as a religious impulse, but also (and for many people, maybe most essentially) a social and communal activity.

But the ground beneath our feet has shifted, and our context has changed. This is true for us, and for other denominations. The Crystal Cathedral, opened in 1980, was the "vanguard of the megachurch movement."[2] But the demographic shift in Orange County, where the cathedral was located, set the stage for its eventual bankruptcy and sale to the Roman Catholic Diocese of Orange County in 2012.[3]

The height of PC(USA) population was 1983. There has been a steady, but gradual decline in membership since then. We have an increasing proportion of small churches, and the definition of what is considered a small church has changed. The 2020 Faith Communities Today survey showed that seventy per cent of faith communities have 100 or fewer weekly attenders.[4] In decades past, a church with 100 or fewer members might have been considered "small," while today many of us would be envious of that number of people in worship. In 2022, the PC(USA) had nearly one-quarter of reporting churches listed as having 0-25 members.[5]

People are no longer Presbyterians just because their parents or grandparents were. They no longer go to worship on Sunday mornings because "that's just what you do."

We may feel like strangers in a strange land, like exiles. Sound familiar? Stanley Hauerwas even titled his 1989 book about mainline Protestants "Resident Aliens," naming out loud the shift and decline.[6]

Adaptive challenges require us to examine the context in which we are currently situated, not where we used to be, or how the world as we knew it once was.

Read Jeremiah 29:4-7

[4] Thus says the LORD of hosts, the God of Israel, to all the exiles whom I have sent into exile from Jerusalem to Babylon: [5] Build houses and live in them; plant gardens and eat what they produce. [6] Take wives and have sons and daughters; take wives for your sons, and give your daughters in marriage, that they may bear sons and daughters; multiply there, and do not decrease. [7] But seek the welfare of the city where I have sent you into exile, and pray to the LORD on its behalf, for in its welfare you will find your welfare.

The people of God have been taken into exile, in Babylon. They are in a land where they do not speak the language. They eat strange foods; they are separated from their homeland and family. They cannot even worship God in the 'correct way,' which is to go to the temple in Jerusalem. They are in a totally unknown and unwanted context. EVERYTHING is different. They have cried out to God for rescue and return.

God's answer? Not what they expected, I bet.

Stay where you are, says God. Settle in and settle down. Raise crops and families. Seek good and not evil, for the context and the place you are in now.

What if you turned to God, right now, and prayed "O God, please change the world…to make it match the way we are used to." How do you think God might respond?

Contexts change. And context matters. And we are called to respond in new, adaptive ways.

John 2:1-10

2 On the third day there was a wedding in Cana of Galilee, and the mother of Jesus was there. [2] Jesus and his disciples had also been invited to the wedding. [3] When the wine gave out, the mother of Jesus said to him, 'They have no wine.' [4] And Jesus said to her, 'Woman, what concern is that to you and to me? My hour has not yet come.' [5] His mother said to the servants, 'Do whatever he tells you.' [6] Now standing there were six stone water-jars for the Jewish rites of purification, each holding twenty or thirty gallons. [7] Jesus said to them, 'Fill the jars with water.' And they filled them up to the brim. [8] He said to them, 'Now draw some out, and take it to the chief steward.' So they took it. [9] When the steward tasted the water that had become

wine, and did not know where it came from (though the
servants who had drawn the water knew), the steward called the
bridegroom [10] *and said to him, 'Everyone serves the good wine*
first, and then the inferior wine after the guests have become
drunk. But you have kept the good wine until now.'

This is the story of the Wedding at Cana. You have probably heard this Scripture previously, perhaps even at a wedding service itself. The context is a wedding celebration, which in Jesus' time and place involved everybody in the village and extended families and could last several days. And then there is a shift in the context. The wedding celebrations are continuing, but Jesus is presented with a problem, brought to his attention by his mother. Jesus, at first, is not aware. "They have no wine," his mom must point out. This would be a "major hospitality blunder."[7] The shame of not being able to provide for all the guests would be noted, and remarked upon, for generations.

In this problematic shift in context, Jesus is clear about what he will, and will not do. He is there as a guest and a member of the community, and nothing more. The fact that Jesus showed up with a bunch of his disciples, (a plus 12 instead of a plus 1!) is not mentioned in the Scripture, only that "Jesus and his disciples 'had also been invited.' Anyone who has more guests—or hungrier and thirstier guests—than they had planned on knows the anxiety this produces.

But after the comment by his mother, Jesus does act. He responds to the change in context. So do the servants, told by Mary "do whatever he tells you."

Now, filling water vessels might seem like the usual task for servants. But they are being told to do this not by the host, nor even by the steward…but by one of the guests. We might see their action as a technical response. But when we are involved in God's adaptive action in a changing context, we are part of a miracle. Note as well that others beside Jesus were involved in this miracle. We will see this again later, as we consider listening to the voices and seeing the talents of others.

Read Acts 6:1-7

Now during those days, when the disciples were increasing in number, the Hellenists complained against the Hebrews because their widows were being neglected in the daily distribution of food. 2 And the twelve called together the whole community of the disciples and said, 'It is not right that we should neglect the word of God in order to wait at tables.[a] 3 Therefore, friends,[b] select from among yourselves seven men of good standing, full of the Spirit and of wisdom, whom we may appoint to this task, 4 while we, for our part, will devote ourselves to prayer and to serving the word.' 5 What they said pleased the whole community, and they chose Stephen, a man full of faith and the Holy Spirit, together with Philip, Prochorus, Nicanor, Timon, Parmenas, and Nicolaus, a proselyte of Antioch. 6 They had these men stand before the apostles, who prayed and laid their hands on them.

7 The word of God continued to spread; the number of the disciples increased greatly in Jerusalem, and a great many of the priests became obedient to the faith.

Soon after Jesus' death, resurrection and ascension, there is already a dissent, a problem. As Matt Skinner writes about life in the early church: "No one ever said this would be easy."[8] Two subgroups in the church are complaining about each other. Remember that these are all Jews in Jerusalem, who follow Jesus as the Messiah. And yet there are cries of "not fair!" The Greek-speaking widows are being neglected in the distribution of food and support.

Some standard, technical responses might have been: Okay, we will take the total number of needy widows, and divide our food share proportionally. Or we will tell those "Others" to quit complaining and just be happy with what they get. Or we will stop the food distribution all together since it has become such a problem.

Have you ever experienced dissension, or cries of "unfair" in your congregation? How was it handled? Our decision making, as Presbyterians, always reflects our theological values. And it relies on discernment. And discernment often calls us to respond adaptively.

We might see this story as a mix of both technical and adaptive responses. Many challenges that come our way require both.

It can be seen as a purely technical response: the community is asked to select some people to equitably serve food. The seven elected have Greek names, and so, it is assumed, will be able to communicate with the Greek-speaking widows. Others will continue to preach and to serve the Word. Two distinct groups, each with a clear mandate and purpose.

Or is it adaptive?

Is this a new way of looking at and responding to a change in the context? Is it lifting up those who serve (which is what the word *diakonos*, from which we get deacons, means) to equal footing with those who preach? Is it a new way to go forward, without neglecting anyone, assigning blame, or having irreconcilable differences within the faith community? Is it an imaginative and creative (and God-blessed) solution to an adaptive challenge?

For we are told: "The word of God continued to spread: the number of disciples increased greatly..." (6: 7)

Questions for discussion:

Imagine you are sent into exile, into an entirely new and unwanted context for your life. When a word from God appears, it is stay here. Make the best of it. Settle in. How would you respond? How do you think the exiles in Babylon felt?

Have you ever faced anything in your life in which you felt an exile/alone/in a totally different context? How did that feel?

What might it mean if God's message to us is to respond adaptively to a change in context? What might that look like for you, or for your family, or for your church?

Was Jesus' action at the wedding in Cana a technical response, an adaptive one…or some combination of both? Explain why you think that.

This was the first of his signs in Cana of Galilee. What other "signs" or miracles are adaptive responses?

Has your congregation ever had disagreements about a previously established ministry/mission/feeding program, etc.?

Have those disagreements been related to changes in context, either in the outer community, or the community inside the congregation? How have they been resolved?

NOTES

1.Gary Vaynerchuk, "Content is King but Context is God," March 21, 2016, accessed November 5, 2023, https://garyvaynerchuk.com/content-is-king-but-context-is-god.

2.Robert P. Jones, *The End of White Christian America* (New York, NY: Simon & Schuster, 2016), 26.

3.Ibid., 28.

4.Hartford Institute for Religious Research, 2020. "Twenty Years of Change: The Faith Communities Today Overview," accessed November 5, 2023, https://faithcommunitiestoday.org/wp-content/uploads/2021/10/Faith-Communities-Today-2020-Summary-Report.pdf.

5.Comparative Summary of Statistics," Office of the General Assembly, PC(U.S.A.), accessed October 23, 2023,
https://pcusa.org/site_media/media/uploads/oga/pdf/statistics/2022_stats_comparativesummaries.pdf.

6.Jones, 213.

7.Karoline M. Lewis, *John* (Minneapolis, MN: Fortress Press, 2014), 38.

8.Matthew L. Skinner, *Intrusive God, Disruptive Gospel* (Grand Rapids, MI: Brazos Press, 2015), 38.

9.Ibid., 39.

Chapter 4

Shifts in Authority

At the time of this writing, I have just returned from attending the Holy Shift! Conference at Montreat Conference Center.

And yes, you can imagine all the word-play jokes that were made with that conference title.

Perhaps this is how you feel in the midst of So. Many. Changes. Holy Shift! is right.

But as we consider adaptive responses, one of the changes will be to make shifts in authority.

And we need to consider those shifts in two different ways.

The first is to reclaim and affirm the Holy Spirit gifts of all members.

The second is to ask ourselves: whose voice have I not heard? Who else do I need to listen to? And by this, I mean not only members and worshippers of our congregations, but perhaps or even especially voices outside our walls, in our community and our world.

While many of us see the pastor as "the expert," the professional Christian, our *PC(USA) Book of Order* reminds us that "through Baptism, the Holy Spirit gives the Church its identity and commissions the

Church for service in the world."[1] That is true for everyone.

And while we do understand the Session (Ruling Elders) as the governing council for the local congregation, "the basic form of ministry is the ministry of the whole people of God."[2] That includes people outside our walls.

At some point you may have been part of a SWOT analysis in your congregation, a gathering at which we talk about Strengths, Weaknesses, Opportunities and Threats facing our church. Often this takes place during a Session retreat, or a long-range planning group meeting. This conversation might be led by an outsider: someone from the Presbytery, or a consultant you have hired. But what we often forget is that what we are hearing is only our own voices, our own ideas, our own views of the church and the world.

But if our ministry context has changed, (and it has), we need to ask: what voices do we need to hear outside our church walls? Who do we need to be in conversation with? At what point(s) do we need to share power and authority? And how do we do that?

The Presbyterian church, in theology and in theory, has always done this.

A Brief Statement of Faith, in the *PC(USA) Book of Confessions* reminds us that the Spirit "calls women and men to all ministries of the church." (10.4) We say that "to each member of Christ's body, the Spirit gives gifts for ministry in the Church and mission in the world."[3]

Who else, then, could we be listening to, talking with? How do we practice the spiritual discipline of listening to others? Who else might have Spirit-given insight for the mission and ministry of your particular congregation? Are there any you think do not have gifts to help the church be the church God is calling us to be? Who do we exclude or ignore? Who is considered too old, too weak, too disabled, too unimportant to be included in discernment? And who has been a surprising voice of wisdom for your congregation?

We often experience this in our personal lives. You might be an expert in some areas: perhaps a seasoned teacher, or master gardener, or talented seamstress. But you also listen to other voices, about areas that you do not know or have expertise in when your car needs work, or you need a heart-valve operation, or your dog is sick.

Tod Bolsinger, in *Canoeing the Mountains*, writes about Lewis and Clark, the Corps of Discovery and the need for an adaptive shift they experienced on their journey. They had planned for a water route to the Pacific. And they traveled as far as they could by canoe…until they reached the Rockies.

In that mountainous terrain, their canoes, their ways of navigating, their maps, all their knowledge and equipment and experience no longer worked in this new context.

To survive and continue their journey, the Corps had to cede some of their educated, white, male roles of authority to a teenage nursing mother, an indigenous female. Sacagawea. She was the one who knew the land, knew how to find and provide food, how to navigate through this particular wilderness. For Lewis and Clark and the Corps, this was a personal and cultural shift.

Christena Cleveland reminds us that "People can meet God within their cultural context, but in order to follow God they must cross into other cultures because that's what Jesus did…Discipleship is cross-cultural."[4] And by this, I mean not just the ethnic/political structures of culture, but the "church culture" that we live in as well.

Numbers 11:24-29

[24] So Moses went out and told the people the words of the LORD; and he gathered seventy elders of the people, and placed them all around the tent. [25] Then the LORD came down in the cloud and spoke to him, and took some of the spirit that was on him and put it on the seventy elders; and when the spirit rested upon them, they prophesied. But they did not do so again.

[26] Two men remained in the camp, one named Eldad, and the other named Medad, and the spirit rested on them; they were among those registered, but they had not gone out to the tent, and so they prophesied in the camp. [27] And a young man ran and told Moses, 'Eldad and Medad are prophesying in the camp.' [28] And Joshua son of Nun, the assistant of Moses, one of his chosen men,[a] said, 'My lord Moses, stop them!' [29] But Moses said to him, 'Are you jealous for my sake? Would that all the LORD's people were prophets, and that the LORD would put his spirit on them!'

Like Lewis and Clark and the Corps of Discovery, the people of God are on a journey through wilderness. In fact, the name for the book of Scripture that we know as "Numbers," is in Hebrew titled "In the Wilderness."[5] And while they are out in that wilderness, there are shifts in context, which require shifts in authority.

The Lord is putting the Holy Spirit on a lot of people: Moses, certainly, and then seventy elders (see v. 25) and then two others.

Eldad and Medad, the two other elders, did not go to the gathering that day. No one knows why, and Scripture doesn't say. Playing hooky? Scared of what might happen when you meet the Living God? Wanted to stay home and watch the game?

But the Spirit rested on them anyway, and they began prophesying. Joshua was fussed about this, but Moses was not. "Would that all the Lord's people were prophets, and that the Lord would put his spirit on them!" (v. 29)

Moses is clearly the leader, and yet he has no problem with others receiving the spirit of the Lord. He has already entrusted leadership to some seventy elders. He "decentralizes," or gives away some of his authority, rightly attributing it to God's spirit.

And while we, as Presbyterians, say that Christ is the Head of the church, and that the discerning body of the local congregation is the Session, we also want to be sure not to, like Joshua, limit who we think God has gifted with the Holy Spirit. When we nominate and elect people for the ministries of Ruling Elder or Deacon in our congregational vote, we might be surprised (in fact, I hope we are) by the diversity of people who are called to these ministries: people of various ages and abilities, genders, occupations and experiences, ethnicities and languages.

We see another instance of God's spirit and discernment coming from an unexpected person, in the story of the healing of Naaman. Another shift in authority, another voice to listen to outside the usual power structures.

2 Kings 5:1-5, 7-15

Naaman, commander of the army of the king of Aram, was a great man and in high favour with his master, because by him the LORD had given victory to Aram. The man, though a mighty warrior, suffered from leprosy.[a] *2 Now the Arameans on one of their raids had taken a young girl captive from the land of Israel, and she served Naaman's wife. 3 She said to her mistress, 'If only my lord were with the prophet who is in Samaria! He would cure him of his leprosy.'*[b] *4 So Naaman*[c] *went in and told his lord just what the girl from the land of Israel had said. 5 And the king of Aram said, 'Go then, and I will send along a letter to the king of Israel.'*

He went, taking with him ten talents of silver, six thousand shekels of gold, and ten sets of garments.

7 When the king of Israel read the letter, he tore his clothes and said, 'Am I God, to give death or life, that this man sends word to me to cure a man of his leprosy?[a] Just look and see how he is trying to pick a quarrel with me.'

8 But when Elisha the man of God heard that the king of Israel had torn his clothes, he sent a message to the king, 'Why have you torn your clothes? Let him come to me, that he may learn that there is a prophet in Israel.' 9 So Naaman came with his horses and chariots, and halted at the entrance of Elisha's house. 10 Elisha sent a messenger to him, saying, 'Go, wash in the Jordan seven times, and your flesh shall be restored and you shall be clean.' 11 But Naaman became angry and went away, saying, 'I thought that for me he would surely come out, and stand and call on the name of the LORD his God, and would wave his hand over the spot, and cure the leprosy![b] 12 Are not Abana[c] and Pharpar, the rivers of Damascus, better than all the waters of Israel? Could I not wash in them, and be clean?' He turned and went away in a rage. 13 But his servants approached and said to him, 'Father, if the prophet had commanded you to do something difficult, would you not have done it? How much more, when all he said to you was, "Wash, and be clean"?' 14 So he went down and immersed himself seven times in the Jordan, according to the word of the man of God; his flesh was restored like the flesh of a young boy, and he was clean.

15 Then he returned to the man of God, he and all his company; he came and stood before him and said, 'Now I know that there is no God in all the earth except in Israel; please accept a present from your servant.'

In your Bible, this story might have the heading of "The Healing of Naaman." I would describe it as a "reluctant" healing.

It is also a story that contains confusion and misdirection. Naaman, a commander in the army of Aram, suffers from leprosy. A young, unnamed enslaved girl speaks to Naaman's wife, and tells her of a "prophet in Samaria," meaning the prophet Elisha. But the word gets passed along to the Naaman, and to the king of Aram, who sends word to the King of Israel…who is distressed to be asked this, for fear of political reprisals from Aram if Naaman is not healed. Elisha the prophet hears of it and sends word for Naaman to wash in the river Jordan seven times, to be cured.

But Naaman, hearing these instructions, is angry, and insulted (there are so many hurt feelings in this story, it's like middle school all over again), but eventually is persuaded to go and wash in the Jordan river…and is healed.

From whom did this word for healing start? An unnamed, enslaved girl. Not someone with power or wealth or authority. It is the people with power who are confused and at a loss. Perhaps the whole threat of political and personal mishaps might have been avoided, if they had listened deeply, and given the enslaved girl's words credence and authority.

Jesus frequently was asked "by what authority" do you do these things/say these things.

We see it in Matthew 21: 23-27, as Jesus is being questioned in the Temple. (see also Mark 11:27-33, Luke 20: 1-8).

And yet, Jesus, while holding all authority in heaven and on earth, shares his power. He says it in Matthew 28:18, but we see it in other places.

Matthew 14:14-16

14 When he went ashore, he saw a great crowd; and he had compassion for them and cured their sick. 15 When it was evening, the disciples came to him and said, 'This is a deserted place, and the hour is now late; send the crowds away so that they may go into the villages and buy food for themselves.' 16 Jesus said to them, 'They need not go away; you give them something to eat.'

At that deserted place (no 7-11's, McDonald's or even grubhub around) the disciples point out to Jesus that the people are hungry. They want Jesus to send the people away. Jesus turns to them and pointedly says "you give them something to eat."

Jesus is not kidding. He fully expects the disciples to get to work. The Greek is in the imperative. It is a command, Jesus is giving away his authority, his blessing, his mercy, to the disciples, for them to share with others. Jesus breaks the bread, but it is the disciples who distribute it. They get to be part of the miracle!

We see the same thing at the end of Matthew, in the Great Commission, where Jesus mentions his own authority...but then commands (again, the imperative) the disciples, as they go out, to make new disciples, to teach and to baptize.

Earlier in the Gospel of Matthew, Jesus had reminded the disciples that whatever they bound on earth, was bound in heaven, and whatever was loosed on earth will be loosed in heaven. (14: 18) Again, Jesus is giving away his authority to the disciples.

This is an adaptive response.

Hunter Farrell and S. Balajiedlang Khyllep, in their recent book *Freeing Congregational Mission*, write about mission not as an enterprise in which American Christians drop in as experts, "fix" something, and then leave, but as an ongoing relationship with partners, based on our mutual relationship with Christ. Which means listening to, being with, and accepting that someone else (not us) would have a better understanding of what is needed, and what would work, in a different context.

Farrell writes: "the upside-down circle of mission companionship requires not merely the presence and participation of those the world considers "weak" and "foolish," but their agency and leadership.[7] It requires humility and true collaboration.

That is a shift in authority. For many of us, it is a difficult move, as it calls us to deeply listen and to let go of our roles as experts.

I want us to revisit the story about the Greek widows that we looked at in the last chapter.

We said that the solution proposed can be seen as a combination of both technical and adaptive responses.

Many challenges do require both kinds of responses. Technical responses utilize and reinforce power and authority wherever it is held or defined in a system.[8] This is part of "that's how we've always done things."

In his book *Intrusive God, Disruptive Gospel*, Matthew Skinner raises a valid question about power dynamics in the Acts 6 Scripture passage. Is the issue that the Greek speaking widows are not getting enough food, or is it that they have been shoved out of the way by a "top down" answer from those (Aramaic/Hebrew speaking men) in authority? Did they take a "job of the community's important food-service ministry away from women and 'institutionalize' it under male overseers?"[9] The grammar in this Scripture passage is not clear.

How might we hear this story differently if the Scripture included an account of the disciples actually going to the Greek-speaking widows to see what they needed, and to consider what agency and authority the women already had in this situation, and then to listen to what views their wisdom and experience gave about viable solutions?

Increasingly, churches are seeking viable solutions for adaptive challenges with their buildings and physical plants. Think about the example listed earlier in this study: a church faces a need for a new roof...but adaptively, begins to ask questions about the underused Sunday School annex, and to look around at the community and see what needs there are. To do that well, they need to be in conversation with community partners, AND they need to listen deeply. Deep listening leads to shifts in authority and to collaboration.

In 2016, Arlington Presbyterian sold its land to Arlington Partnership for Affordable Housing. A 173-unit affordable housing space, called Gilliam Place, was built on the former church site. The congregation continues to exist and thrive, using space on the ground floor of that building.
(https://arlingtonpresbyterian.org/our-vision/)

But the conversations and deep listening began to take place long before that, as church members both observed, and heard from their neighbors, that people who worked in that area could not afford to live there. Affordable housing was a real need but was not accessible for most.

The Session, pastor and congregation had to look outside their own walls and listen to voices that were not their own. They had to cede some authority and listen to people who knew the area and knew the needs of the community. They had to collaborate, as a congregation with other community partners and agencies, to do this new thing they believed God was calling them to.

These shifts in authority, both within the congregation, and between the congregation and the outside ministry context, are not simply organizational change, which would be a technical response. Rather, they require a shift not only in authority but also in culture. Culture is "the norms of behavior and the shared values in a group of people."[10] Unfortunately, culture also often operates as "the unspoken rules" of a system. That is, you might not know what the rules are, until you break them. As Peter Drucker, management consultant has famously said, "Culture eats strategy for breakfast," meaning, all the strategic plans in the world won't change the culture of a congregation or organization. What does change culture? It is our hearts engaging in discernment, deep listening, and taking small steps in partnership with the larger community.

Roxburgh and Romanuk, in *The Missional Leader*, tell the story of an aging congregation whose ministry context was changing around them. Sound familiar? Some members of this congregation began to realize that the church had become "an island of white members in an increasingly multiracial community."[11] The congregation members went to the neighborhood associations with ideas for improving the area. Unsurprisingly, their suggestions were ignored or rebuffed. The group then began to simply act: to pick up litter that they found at the side of the street, every Tuesday and Thursday. Their small actions spoke more loudly than their words. They were invited into the store of a local owner who previously had told the congregation members to leave and not come back. Seeing their activity, while at the same time NOT receiving any further "advice" from the church members began to open the way for dialogue and friendship. The congregation members had to earn trust, but also had to begin to listen, to give up some authority, in order to engage in relationships and listening with others.

Questions for discussion:

Why do you think people did not really listen to the enslaved girl? What happens when people with no authority speak the truth...and are not heeded? Has this ever happened to you, or have you seen this in your community?

Was this an adaptive challenge for Naaman? What was Naaman's first reaction/proposed solution? How did he respond?

"You give them something to eat." Jesus tells the disciples. Note that in Matthew's version of this feeding, there is not even a little boy with a small number of fish and bread, just the disciples.

What does it mean for us when Jesus uses a command? How do we respond?

Is this understanding of the complaint in Acts 6 new to you? Tell the story in a way that includes the action and agency of the Greek-speaking widows.

Does this telling feel different? If so, in what ways?

Activity:

Think about your congregation, its setting, and what—and who and is not—around it. Take a walk around the outside, or a short drive around the area/neighborhood. What do you see? What stands out to you?

Has that changed over the years? How much conversation does the church have with its neighbors?

Its community? What are the deep needs of the people around you?

How can you find out?

NOTES

1.*PC(U.S.A.), Book of Order 2023-2025*, (Louisville: KY, Office of the General Assembly), W-3.0402, 95.

2.Ibid., G-2.0101, 25.

3.Ibid., W-1.0105, 78.

4.Christena Cleveland, *Disunity in Christ: Uncovering the Hidden Forces That Keep Us Apart* (Downers Grove, IL: InterVarsity Press, 2013), 21.

5.Adele Berlin and Marc Zvi Brettler, eds., *The Jewish Study Bible* (Oxford University Press, New York, NY: 2004), 281.

6.Frank Yamada, "Commentary on Numbers 11:4-6, 10-16, 24-29," Working Preacher, September 27, 2009, accessed October 25, 2023, workingpreacher.org.

7. B. Hunter Farrell and S. Balajiedlang Khyllep, *Freeing Congregational Mission* (Downer's Grove, IL: InterVarsity Press, 2022), 68.

8.Heifetz, Linsky, Grashow, T*he Practice of Adaptive Leadership*, 20.

9.Matthew L. Skinner, Intr*usive God, Disruptive Gospel*, (Grand Rapids, MI: Brazos Press, 2015), 39.

10. John P. Kotter, T*he Heart of Change* (Boston, MA: Harvard Business Review Press, 2002),163.

11.Alan J. Roxburgh and Fred Romanuk, *The Missional Leader* (San Francisco, CA: Jossey Bass, Inc, 2006), 68.

Chapter Five

Risk and loss and failure...oh my!

I am what is known as a "middle to late adopter." This means that while I might hear about the latest iPhone or car or coffee grinder/brewer/slicer/dicer, I will not buy one, until I see and hear other's experiences with those items. I don't want to be the first to try something, but I might like to be one of the next.

People who study change in organizations say that there is always a diversity in how, when, or even if, people embrace change. Some are early adopters; some, like me, are middle to late adopters. And some are never adopters: solid "no's," or even "over my dead body, no." No matter what the issue is, some do not want change.

The same is true for our congregations. The funny part is that while we might know, intellectually, a change is needed, or even that change is the only alternative we have, because we can see that what have been doing all along is no longer working (a sure sign you are facing an adaptive challenge), we will still resist change.

People resist change when we fear the losses the change will bring. Technical changes don't stir up these feelings of fear and loss, since they really are just doing what we have always done.

The truth is that change is hardly ever (maybe never) a win-win situation. All change begins with an ending, and all change, even good or wanted change, involves some kind of loss. And loss is almost always accompanied by grief, and perhaps lament. The largest category of the Psalms are lament psalms. As people of God, we have a Scriptural model to use in our grief over loss and changing context. But we must be clear: naming the loss and bringing our grief to God is not the same as getting stuck. And while our grief may provoke in us denial and anger, even emotional distress and conflict, the psalms of lament most frequently turn, at the end, to hope, and to change. Grief may push us back into technical solutions. Any transition may push us into those responses, but "the first phase of transition begins when people identify what they are losing and learn how to manage those losses."[1]

I am not sure we have yet learned to name our losses out loud, much less 'manage' them. We are relying on unchanging patterns and habits rather than flexibility to meet new challenges. We would do anything to keep the old systems and practices in place. So, as the church, we resist change.

All that resistance to change can prevent us from following Christ faithfully.

I want to affirm that church people are good, faithful people, and we want to be good stewards of all that God has given us. I find this especially true for Elders, Deacons and Trustees. We don't want to make choices or take actions that might harm what has been entrusted to our care, whether that is finances, a building, a program, or people. We feel a fiduciary responsibility in our ministry, and so we shy away from risk, even "necessary risks," as Teri McDowell Ott names them.

Frankly, we don't want to risk failure. Some of us live in congregations with long memories, in which stories are told forever. You might know some of them. They sound like this: "Remember that time Dale took over the BBQ and everybody got food poisoning? Don't let Dale near the kitchen ever again!" That story lives on, and that was more than two decades ago.

Culturally we are told "Failure is not an option."[2] Technology firms tell their employees that if they are not failing, they are not being creative enough. If we are to risk faithful adaptive change, then we must be willing to know that "Failure is always an option," as Adam Savage of *Mythbusters* has stated.[3] Maybe real failure is the refusal to take risks. Learning from failure, no matter what the outcome, means it is not failure at all. Creativity cannot exist when there is fear of, or punishment for, failure.

Daniel Pink, in a commencement address at Northwestern University, said that we need to "burst the double bubble of comfort and convention and just do stuff, even if you don't know precisely where it's going to lead … This might sound risky. And you know what? It is. It is really risky. But the greater risk is to choose false certainty over genuine ambiguity."[4]

We are not comfortable with ambiguity. But sometimes our resistance is based not on ambiguity, but on misremembering.

Exodus 16:1-3

16 The whole congregation of the Israelites set out from Elim; and Israel came to the wilderness of Sin, which is between Elim and Sinai, on the fifteenth day of the second month after they had departed from the land of Egypt. ² The whole congregation of the Israelites complained against Moses and Aaron in the wilderness. ³ The Israelites said to them, 'If only we had died by the hand of the LORD in the land of Egypt, when we sat by the fleshpots and ate our fill of bread; for you have brought us out into this wilderness to kill this whole assembly with hunger.'

The people are complaining so soon after being freed by God. And their complaint doesn't sound like the memories of those who had been so recently enslaved.

They have been set free. But now, six weeks later, in the middle of the wilderness, the people begin to remember "the good old days." Which, frankly, were not that good. Not good at all; so much so that they cried to the Lord, and to Moses, for rescue. And yet here they are, talking about all the good food they had to eat, back in Egypt. Our memories of the good old days might not be entirely accurate. It is difficult to remember clearly, to see clearly, into the past.

Sometimes resistance to change comes from the sheer amount of effort that overcoming complacency and habit takes. We might know the change is necessary, but we just don't have the energy.

I was once with a congregation who told me in our meeting that they wanted to change, in order to revitalize. But after the meeting, several different people pulled me aside in the parking lot. And while everyone there at the meeting had all nodded their heads "yes," to the revitalization plans, once outside, they told me a different story: that they were old, and tired, and in fact "we spend most of our time going to doctor's appointments." That was the real state of that congregation: they did not have the energy or capacity to change adaptively.

And often, resistance to change comes not from lack of energy, but from fear of loss.

Matthew 16:13-16, then 21-23

13 Now when Jesus came into the district of Caesarea Philippi, he asked his disciples, 'Who do people say that the Son of Man is?' 14 And they said, 'Some say John the Baptist, but others Elijah, and still others Jeremiah or one of the prophets.' 15 He said to them, 'But who do you say that I am?' 16 Simon Peter answered, 'You are the Messiah,[a] the Son of the living God.'

21 From that time on, Jesus began to show his disciples that he must go to Jerusalem and undergo great suffering at the hands of the elders and chief priests and scribes, and be killed, and on the third day be raised. 22 And Peter took him aside and began to rebuke him, saying, 'God forbid it, Lord! This must never happen to you.' 23 But he turned and said to Peter, 'Get behind me, Satan! You are a stumbling-block to me; for you are setting your mind not on divine things but on human things.'

Peter, in a moment of Holy Spirit enlightenment, blurts out who Jesus is: The Messiah, the Son of the Living God. And yet, just a few verses later, when Jesus explains to the disciples what that will mean, Peter is shocked and appalled. He rejects not only what Jesus is saying, but also cannot bend his thinking and expectations around what the Messiah is and will be. He cannot imagine any other ways for the Son of God to be other than triumphant and victorious. Any other way would be loss and grief: the loss of friend and teacher, the loss of power and authority, the loss of identity as Peter knows it.

Luke 18:18-23

18 A certain ruler asked him, 'Good Teacher, what must I do to inherit eternal life?' 19 Jesus said to him, 'Why do you call me good? No one is good but God alone. 20 You know the commandments: "You shall not commit adultery; You shall not murder; You shall not steal; You shall not bear false witness; Honour your father and mother."' 21 He replied, 'I have kept all these since my youth.' 22 When Jesus heard this, he said to him, 'There is still one thing lacking. Sell all that you own and distribute the money to the poor, and you will have treasure in heaven; then come, follow me.' 23 But when he heard this, he became sad; for he was very rich.

"The Rich Young Ruler" asks Jesus how to inherit eternal life. He is not happy with the answer he receives. This story appears in all three Synoptic Gospels. In Luke's version, the man is described as both rich, and a ruler. The Greek says that he should sell all he has and distribute it to the poor, an action that would change him, and his community. To follow Jesus' instructions would mean that he will lose both his wealth and his standing in the community. He goes away "very sad." The Greek word there can mean to be grieved, even to the point of death. But it was a kind of death, a death of social status and identity, that the rich man was trying to avoid.

Our resistance to change can be founded in fear of a loss of our own identity. Many times, this does not even reach the level of conscious thought. But the question is there: who will I be, if I am not the beloved Sunday School director? Who will I be if I am no longer able to do the spring chicken BBQ? And who will we be, if our church is no longer "the BIG church" in town, the one with community leaders and prominent citizens and full to bursting Sunday School classrooms?

Matthew 25:14-30[5]

[14] *For it is as if a man, going on a journey, summoned his slaves and entrusted his property to them;* [15] *to one he gave five talents,[a] to another two, to another one, to each according to his ability. Then he went away.* [16] *The one who had received the five talents went off at once and traded with them, and made five more talents.* [17] *In the same way, the one who had the two talents made two more talents.* [18] *But the one who had received the one talent went off and dug a hole in the ground and hid his master's money.* [19] *After a long time the master of those slaves came and settled accounts with them.* [20] *Then the one who had received the five talents came forward, bringing five more talents, saying, "Master, you handed over to me five talents; see, I have made five more talents."* [21] *His master said to him, "Well done, good and trustworthy slave; you have been trustworthy in a few*

78

things, I will put you in charge of many things; enter into the joy of your master." ²² And the one with the two talents also came forward, saying, "Master, you handed over to me two talents; see, I have made two more talents." ²³ His master said to him, "Well done, good and trustworthy slave; you have been trustworthy in a few things, I will put you in charge of many things; enter into the joy of your master." ²⁴ Then the one who had received the one talent also came forward, saying, "Master, I knew that you were a harsh man, reaping where you did not sow, and gathering where you did not scatter seed; ²⁵ so I was afraid, and I went and hid your talent in the ground. Here you have what is yours." ²⁶ But his master replied, "You wicked and lazy slave! You knew, did you, that I reap where I did not sow, and gather where I did not scatter? ²⁷ Then you ought to have invested my money with the bankers, and on my return I would have received what was my own with interest. ²⁸ So take the talent from him, and give it to the one with the ten talents. ²⁹ For to all those who have, more will be given, and they will have an abundance; but from those who have nothing, even what they have will be taken away. ³⁰ As for this worthless slave, throw him into the outer darkness, where there will be weeping and gnashing of teeth."

We know this as the Parable of the Talents. A talent was a unit of money equal to between 10- and 20-years' income. So, a lot. The master, we find out, is a less than honorable guy. It is no wonder the slave entrusted with one talent does not dare risk even that small (compared to the other slaves) amount of money. In The Message version of this parable, the word "risk" is used in v. 28-30: "Take the thousand and give it to the one who risked the most."⁶ The master in this parable rewards the two slaves who took risks. But is this risk built on an unjust system? How do we know which risks to take? What would have happened if the slaves in this story had risked, and failed?

Adaptive change involves risk, loss and failure. To the Roman/Greek world, Jesus' life and death were seen as failures. No story of a successful leader would include being publicly executed by the Romans. What kind of a Messiah would that be? A failed one.

Sometimes, though, we are willing to take risks and perhaps fail because we are pushed to it. We have run out of options, a sure sign that we are facing an adaptive challenge. We are desperate and will try just about anything. And if that means taking a risk, then so be it.

Luke 8:40-42a, 8:43-48, 49-56

40 Now when Jesus returned, the crowd welcomed him, for they were all waiting for him. 41 Just then there came a man named Jairus, a leader of the synagogue. He fell at Jesus' feet and begged him to come to his house, 42 for he had an only daughter, about twelve years old, who was dying.

43 Now there was a woman who had been suffering from haemorrhages for twelve years; and though she had spent all she had on physicians,[a] no one could cure her. 44 She came up behind him and touched the fringe of his clothes, and immediately her haemorrhage stopped. 45 Then Jesus asked, 'Who touched me?' When all denied it, Peter[b] said, 'Master, the crowds surround you and press in on you.' 46 But Jesus said, 'Someone touched me; for I noticed that power had gone out from me.' 47 When the woman saw that she could not remain hidden, she came trembling; and falling down before him, she declared in the presence of all the people why she had touched him, and how she had been immediately healed. ⁴⁸ He said to her, 'Daughter, your faith has made you well; go in peace.'

As he went, the crowds pressed in on him.

⁴⁹ While he was still speaking, someone came from the leader's house to say, 'Your daughter is dead; do not trouble the teacher any longer.' ⁵⁰ When Jesus heard this, he replied, 'Do not fear. Only believe, and she will be saved.' ⁵¹ When he came to the house, he did not allow anyone to enter with him, except Peter, John, and James, and the child's father and mother. ⁵² They were all weeping and wailing for her; but he said, 'Do not weep; for she is not dead but sleeping.' ⁵³ And they laughed at him, knowing that she was dead. ⁵⁴ But he took her by the hand and called out, 'Child, get up!' ⁵⁵ Her spirit returned, and she got up at once. Then he directed them to give her something to eat. ⁵⁶ Her parents were astounded; but he ordered them to tell no one what had happened.

These two stories of healing, sandwiched together, are both stories of people who are desperate. So desperate that they are willing to risk everything, to lose their identity, perhaps to be shamed, fired, or even killed, in order to gain healing.

Jairus is the leader, the "president" of the synagogue, a man with social status and power. And yet, when his daughter is dying, he reaches out to Jesus, a rabbi operating outside the regular system of religion and healing. Jairus would do anything, go to anyone to help his child, even if it meant the loss of his place and social identity and employment in the synagogue.

The unnamed "woman with a hemorrhage," as she is commonly known, is at a similar crisis point. She has been suffering for twelve years and has spent all her means on physicians and cures and is only worse. Upon hearing about Jesus, the woman goes out into public, risking punishment, perhaps even being stoned by the crowd, as she was ritually "impure" from her bleeding and should not be out in public. And yet she went, thinking, perhaps, either I will be cured, or I will be killed. Either way, I am not going to go home the same.

Both people show radical adaptive change in this moment. They are risking their own identity and place in the community, and for the woman, perhaps even her own life. Crisis can push us to radical adaptive change.

We can have the pain of staying the same, or the pain of change.

Some people put the choice to the church even more bluntly: Change. Or die.

Questions for Discussion:

How do you feel about risk? for yourself, for your church?

What is the difference (is there a difference?) in "stepping out in faith" and taking a risk? What does the Parable of the Talents teach us about risk?

Thomas Aquinas observed that "if the highest aim of a captain were to preserve the ship, the captain would keep it in port forever."[7] How does that apply to the church? The life of faith?

Think about all the people in the Bible who risked. Which ones, if any, grab your attention and imagination? Would you have acted like Abram and Sarai did? Like the rich young ruler? Like the woman with a hemorrhage?

Give an example of a failure you experienced. What did you learn from it?

Has your church ever experienced a crisis which required an urgent change? If you feel comfortable, please share what that was, and what the outcome was.

Have you ever experienced a time when it was change…or die?

NOTES

1. William Bridges, "Bridges Transition Model," William Bridges Associates, (blog) accessed November 30, 2023, https://wmbridges.com/about/what-is-transition/.

2. Gene Kranz, *Failure Is Not an Option* (New York, NY: Simon & Schuster, 2009).

3. Adam Savage, Mythbusters, Discovery Channel, accessed March 13, 2020, https://go.discovery.com/tv-shows/mythbusters/.

4. Maria Popova, "Why the Best Roadmap to an Interesting Life Is the One You Make Up as You Go Along: Daniel Pink's Commencement Address," the marginalian (blog), June 25, 2014, accessed November 30,2023, https://www.themarginalian.org/2014/06/25/daniel-pink-northwestern-commencement/.

5. Thanks to Rev. Gail Henderson-Belsito and the Adult Bible Study of Caldwell Presbyterian Church, for their thoughts and discussion on this parable.

6. Eugene H. Peterson, *The Message Remix*, (Colorado Springs, CO: Navpres, 2003), 1813.

7. Nick Carter, "Adaptive Leadership: Planning in a Time of Transition," *Theological Education*, Volume 46, 2 (2011): 7-13.

Chapter Six

Same and different, all at the same time

Change…or die.

I said in the previous chapter that is the choice facing congregations, and our denomination.

Sometimes, change does feel like dying. Sometimes, to be honest, we do need to let some things die.

But by the grace of God, our foundational faith story is about death.

And also, new life. In Christ, there is always newness of life.

But we forget that the death part comes first.

Death always precedes resurrection. Always.

And we don't like that. Adaptive change will require some things to die away, so that we can live anew.

In a technical response to an adaptive challenge, we keep trying the same old solutions. In an adaptive change, we try a shift, a new paradigm, a new way of thinking and approaching and asking different questions.

As we begin to embrace and live into adaptive changes, we notice that on the other side of that new thing, are elements that are the same, recognizable, continuous, as well as things that are new. We do not need to throw the baby out with the bathwater. But we also need to be clear about what to jettison, what to forsake (to use language of the King James Bible), that is getting in the way of our following Christ.

In the post-resurrection accounts, on the other side of the disruptive, radical, miraculous, adaptive change of the resurrection, there are elements that are the same, and at the same time, also different.

As you read, notice how the disciples, who knew and loved and studied and traveled with Jesus, do not always recognize him.

Notice, also, the things that are the same: speaking, feeding, being with, comforting and blessing.

Luke 24:13-17, 30-31

13 Now on that same day two of them were going to a village called Emmaus, about seven miles *from Jerusalem,* *14 and talking with each other about all these things that had happened.* *15 While they were talking and discussing, Jesus himself came near and went with them,* *16 but their eyes were kept from recognizing him.* *17 And he said to them, 'What are you discussing with each other while you walk along?' They stood still, looking sad.*

30 When he was at the table with them, he took bread, blessed and broke it, and gave it to them. *31 Then their eyes were opened, and they recognized him; and he vanished from their sight.*

It is Easter evening, although the two people walking from Jerusalem don't really understand that yet. As they are walking, they are talking, I think passionately, about "all these things that had happened," which is a pretty dry summary of Jesus' crucifixion, the three days, and the empty tomb. While they are walking and talking (the word here means something like tossing back and forth), a person appears along the road, whom they do not recognize.

As this stranger accompanies them on their walk, he explains the Scriptures to them. It is not until mealtime, with the blessing, breaking and giving of bread, that their eyes are opened, and they recognize Jesus. That is the contiguous part. Even on this other side of such a radical and adaptive change, feeding and blessing and giving continue. The very nature of God who feeds and saves is present and intact and unchanging, even in this post-cataclysmic time for them.

So what did they do? They ran back to tell the others in Jerusalem. Not where they were planning on going that evening. Another change.

John 20:19-22

19 When it was evening on that day, the first day of the week, and the doors of the house where the disciples had met were locked for fear of the Jews, Jesus came and stood among them and said, 'Peace be with you.' 20 After he said this, he showed them his hands and his side. Then the disciples rejoiced when they saw the Lord. 21 Jesus said to them again, 'Peace be with you. As the Father has sent me, so I send you.' 22 When he had

*said this, he breathed on them and said to them, 'Receive the
Holy Spirit.*

After the death of Jesus, and the discovery of the
empty tomb, the disciples are together behind closed
doors, locked in out of fear. And Jesus comes to them,
where they are. He blesses them, and even offers his
own body for them to see as evidence that it is actually
and physically him. His body retains the marks of the
crucifixion; his blessing continues with his words of
peace, previously spoken to them in John 14.

John 21:4-7, 12-14

*4 Just after daybreak, Jesus stood on the beach; but the disciples
did not know that it was Jesus. 5 Jesus said to them, 'Children,
you have no fish, have you?' They answered him, 'No.' 6 He
said to them, 'Cast the net to the right side of the boat, and you
will find some.' So they cast it, and now they were not able to
haul it in because there were so many fish. 7 That disciple
whom Jesus loved said to Peter, 'It is the Lord!' When Simon
Peter heard that it was the Lord, he put on some clothes, for he
was naked, and jumped into the lake.*

*¹² Jesus said to them, 'Come and have breakfast.' Now none of
the disciples dared to ask him, 'Who are you?' because they
knew it was the Lord. ¹³ Jesus came and took the bread and
gave it to them, and did the same with the fish. ¹⁴ This was now
the third time that Jesus appeared to the disciples after he was
raised from the dead.*

This is one of my favorite Scriptures, and not only
because I relish a good breakfast after working all
night. The disciples have gone home to Galilee and

have gone back to doing the only thing they know, which is fishing. The risk that they took following Jesus looks like failure. And when they do go back to fishing, even that is a failure, too. They fished all night and caught nothing. But there is Jesus, (at this point unrecognized) making breakfast for them! Again, we see the continuity of a God who provides, even after risk and loss and seeming failure. They fish, and now receive abundance. God's provision and abundance (remember, John is the Gospel in which we hear the story of the wedding at Cana—all that wine! The best wine! And so much of it!) continue, even in a new situation and adaptive challenge.

Note verse 12b: "now none of them dared to ask him "who are you?" because they knew it was the Lord."

When we go through adaptive change as congregations, there will be things that will be the same, and things that will be different. In adaptive change, we can both retain our foundational stories and values and explore new ways of being. The key is to find out which parts of our history and shared practice still give life, still align with the Incarnational God we worship.

Our foundational theologies and values remain the same, but they might be expressed and lived out in different ways. Our gathering as a worshipping community might remain the same but might happen in a new space or time or way.

And the things that we love, and cherish, and know? We might need to let go of some of them.

Phyllis Tickle, in her book *The Great Emergence*, uses the image of a church rummage sale.[1] Just as Jesus says in a parable (Matthew 13: 51-52), we are to bring out our treasures, old and new, and reexamine them. What no longer fits? And what do we discover we need to keep? Are there any old "treasures" we discover anew?

South Presbyterian Church in Rochester, New York, is an historic congregation. With roots beginning in 1849, a building and a life together grew. But as in so many churches, in the late 20th century, the congregation was growing older, and smaller. The city of Rochester had changed around them.

A season of discernment was called for. At the beginning of this discernment process, an elder stood up and said "We simply cannot get rid of our building. It is who we are." Five years later, after much prayer, study, and discernment, which included seeking together with another congregation, the Presbytery of Geneva, and their neighborhood, that same Elder said "We have to get rid of our building. It is getting in the way of our mission." South Presbyterian developed Acts of Faith groups, responding to needs in the community. They meet in new spaces, hold Bible studies in coffee shops, and lead worship in a skilled nursing facility. They had 20 Acts of Faith groups in 2019, with a Church membership of 58. But 5,926 different people participate in at least one Act of Faith at least once that year, and 25,399 contacts with people in the community were made, each time "bumping up against the Love of the Risen Christ through us."[2]

Do you see how things are both the same, and different, on the other side of South Presbyterian's adaptive response? They still worship, but in a different space, and with a different, larger community. They still study Scripture; they are still following Jesus and sharing the good news, just in new ways. All along the way, their prayer has been: "Put us where you want us and show us what to do."[3]

Questions for discussion:

Think about the post-resurrection stories: What is the same? What is different? Think about the changes your congregation has made, whatever they were. How much was carried over from previous values/behaviors? What changed? What stayed the same? Are there things your congregation simply cannot change because you cannot be who you are, without them? But are there also things you MUST change, in order to be who you are as a congregation and follower of Christ?

If comfortable, share a time when you have experienced a deep change in your life, maybe even failure. What was life like on the other side of it? Were there things that remained the same, even after the event? What were they? Where was God in those moments for you?

NOTES

1.Phyllis Tickle, *The Great Emergence* (Grand Rapids, MI: Baker Books, 2008).

2.South Presbyterian Church, "History Summary-2," https://southpc.org/wp-content/uploads/2023/08/History-Summary-2.pdf, accessed October 29, 2023.

3. Ibid.

Chapter Seven

Time, community, flexibility, and courage

If adaptive change is a change in beliefs habits, loyalties and priorities, (and we keep saying it is) that change may happen instantly...or over a period of time.

We all have heard stories of someone's crystal clear, one point in time, coming to Jesus moment. Perhaps that is your personal experience of faith.

Certainly, we saw this in Peter's declaration of "You are the Messiah, the son of the Living God" in Matthew 16. Peter had startling clarity in that moment.

Saul's journey of faith has some similarities and some differences with Peter's experience. Saul, breathing threats, was headed to Jerusalem, and was hoping to bring men and women followers of Jesus along the way for religious trial. Suddenly "a light from heaven flashed around him, and he heard a voice." (Acts 9: 1-5) Saul had this moment of clarity.

But Saul then spends the next three days without sight, neither eating or drinking but trying, presumably, to come to grips with what had just happened, and who he knew himself, and God, to be.

And while we might think of Saul/Paul as a hard-charging, full speed ahead kind of guy, and we have the account in Acts of Paul preaching "immediately" while in Damascus after the scales fell from his eyes, we also have Paul's letter to the church in Galatia, in which he says he "went away into Arabia, and afterwards I returned to Damascus." (Gal 1:17)

Debate remains over which is the more "correct" timeline, and what Paul was doing during that time, but there seems to be a point at which Paul needed to stop, and consider, and process everything that has happened to him.

Paul, then, seems to have been in some kind of state, whether a literal, physical "Arabia," or a spiritual wilderness, in which he needed time to reflect on his personal experience, and on the large gap between what he had previously believed and acted upon, and what he has experienced and now knows, which will include large shifts in his beliefs and loyalties. As we have said, on the other side of the adaptive change there are elements that are both same and different, so also there is both continuity and discontinuity in Paul's relating of his experience and his commission to preach.[1] Adaptive change responses can be immediate, or happen over time, or not at all.

Acts 17:22-32

Then Paul stood in front of the Areopagus and said,
'Athenians, I see how extremely religious you are in every
way. ²³ For as I went through the city and looked carefully at

the objects of your worship, I found among them an altar with the inscription, "To an unknown god." What therefore you worship as unknown, this I proclaim to you. [24] *The God who made the world and everything in it, he who is Lord of heaven and earth, does not live in shrines made by human hands,* [25] *nor is he served by human hands, as though he needed anything, since he himself gives to all mortals life and breath and all things.* [26] *From one ancestor* [a] *he made all nations to inhabit the whole earth, and he allotted the times of their existence and the boundaries of the places where they would live,* [27] *so that they would search for God* [b] *and perhaps grope for him and find him—though indeed he is not far from each one of us.* [28] *For "In him we live and move and have our being"; as even some of your own poets have said,*

"For we too are his offspring."

[29] *Since we are God's offspring, we ought not to think that the deity is like gold, or silver, or stone, an image formed by the art and imagination of mortals.* [30] *While God has overlooked the times of human ignorance, now he commands all people everywhere to repent,* [31] *because he has fixed a day on which he will have the world judged in righteousness by a man whom he has appointed, and of this he has given assurance to all by raising him from the dead.'*

[32] *When they heard of the resurrection of the dead, some scoffed; but others said, 'We will hear you again about this.'*

This is Paul's speech at the Areopagus in Athens. Paul gives a compelling speech, gathering together what two groups of disparate cultures have in common, and testifying to the resurrection of Christ from the dead. But, despite Paul's rhetoric, we are told, "some scoffed...and others said, "We will hear you again about this." The Athenians are not, at this point, able to make that adaptive change, to give up what they know and are comfortable with, to embrace the Risen Lord whom Paul is preaching. But they also do not (at least some of them) close the door to that possibility. We might describe them as "late adopters" of change. In his book *Choosing Change*, Peter Coutts writes that there will always be some who are early adopters, some who are middle to late adopters, some who will adopt change if you address their specific issues (usually around loss) and some, who frankly, will be "never adopters."

John 3:1-9

Now there was a Pharisee named Nicodemus, a leader of the Jews. [2] He came to Jesus[a] by night and said to him, 'Rabbi, we know that you are a teacher who has come from God; for no one can do these signs that you do apart from the presence of God.' [3] Jesus answered him, 'Very truly, I tell you, no one can see the kingdom of God without being born from above.[b] [4] Nicodemus said to him, 'How can anyone be born after having grown old? Can one enter a second time into the mother's womb and be born?' [5] Jesus answered, 'Very truly, I tell you, no one can enter the kingdom of God without being born of water and Spirit. [6] What is born of the flesh is flesh, and what is born of the Spirit is spirit.[c] [7] Do not be astonished that I said to you, "You[d] must be born from above."[e] [8] The wind[f] blows where it chooses, and you hear the sound of it, but you do not know where it comes from or where it goes. So it is with everyone who is born of the Spirit.' [9] Nicodemus said to him, 'How can these things be?'

This is the beginning of the story of Nicodemus. A Pharisee, a leader of the Jews, Nicodemus comes to see Jesus by night. Think about the possible risk and loss to Nicodemus here, going to see someone who is outside the Jewish religious establishment, and seen perhaps as an instigator against Rome. Nicodemus respectfully addresses Jesus as Rabbi, asks a question, and is given an answer he cannot comprehend. He just cannot seem to change his mind about this.

John 19:38-40

After these things, Joseph of Arimathea, who was a disciple of Jesus, though a secret one because of his fear of the Jews, asked Pilate to let him take away the body of Jesus. Pilate gave him permission; so he came and removed his body. [39] Nicodemus, who had at first come to Jesus by night, also came, bringing a mixture of myrrh and aloes, weighing about a hundred pounds. [40] They took the body of Jesus and wrapped it with the spices in linen cloths, according to the burial custom of the Jews.

Nicodemus appears again after Jesus' death by crucifixion. Lest we forget, Scripture reminds us he is "[the one] who came to Jesus by night." Nicodemus brings a huge, costly amount of myrrh and aloes to care for Jesus' body, enough for 75 bodies, by one account. We do not know Nicodemus' thought or belief in Jesus. Scripture never explicitly states that Nicodemus became a follower of Jesus. Yet here he is, with an extravagant, abundant supply. Perhaps it has taken Nicodemus all this time to make an adaptive change? Perhaps he is still in the middle of that change?

An adaptive response might fluctuate. Peter, who was so adamant about who Jesus was, the Messiah, (Matthew 16: 16) is also the same one who very quickly (Matthew 16:23) resists Jesus' description of what the Messiah will have to undergo. Peter is resisting both what a proper "Messiah" will look like/act, but also, perhaps, fears what that risk that will mean for him as a follower of Jesus.

Peter denies Jesus three times in the night before Jesus' crucifixion. His previous impulsive testimony and insight don't seem to have had any lasting effect. And yet, we later find Peter fishing at the shore of Galilee when Jesus appears, and it is Peter who, upon hearing someone say, "It is the Lord," jumps into the water and wades in to greet him. Shortly after this, Peter says three times how much he loves Jesus.

We might see Peter's trajectory as waffling, or indecisiveness, or as gradually growing into adaptive responses. He shows us a first, impulsive adaptive response, and then backtracking, and then, finally, aligning himself with the adaptive change of Jesus as Messiah and Lord.

Adaptive change may happen rapidly or may take time, but will require flexibility.

One of the aspects of faith communities that is so important, but is not often talked about, is flexibility. In the same way a body needs to be flexible to be healthy, the body of Christ, the church, also needs to be flexible.

However, this doesn't mean "anything goes"! It does mean, though, that the ability to change without breaking, which is the difference between being flexible and rigid, is an important quality for a congregation.

Flexibility can be described as a person's or community's "preference for change."[2] Successful adaptive solutions require and employ "an ethic of ingenuity [which] is fundamentally flexible in nature."[3] But any church's openness to change is "more than a matter of congregational preference or going along with social trends; it reflects the ongoing divine-human call and response present in every person's life and every community's history."[4]

And while it may be (slightly) easier to be flexible all by yourself, encouraging and growing a readiness for change and openness to try new things is more cumbersome in a community. Think about how difficult (or not) it might be to get your entire family to try something new for Thanksgiving dinner, much less ask the church to make changes.

Flexibility can be fostered by trying new things "for a season," and by starting small. The ability and attitude to embrace adaptive change is vital to a transformative and transforming a congregation, as flexibility allows for innovation as new contexts emerge.[5]

The youth at a church in Sacramento started something new, an intergenerational bread baking ministry. They applied for, and received a grant, organized, and bought flour in bulk. The flour, being organic, would expire in a few days, and so needed to be used quickly.

And then the Covid hit, and the city of Sacramento shut down.

The youth and church were able to pivot, even when they had not planned to, with all that soon-to-expire flour. They reached out to community partners and families and distributed some of the flour. They baked muffins, and other baked goods. They baked the communion bread that was used in the church's first virtual communion celebration. They remained flexible and were able to innovate and respond to a shifting context.[6]

Many of us, however, will find ourselves at a point at which the adaptive challenge is so large, or urgent, that the time for small steps toward flexibility is past.

Leadership for adaptive change needs to be housed not in just one person (the pastor) or groups of people (the Session). That means that we all need to be flexible…and courageous. There will be times when we have to say difficult things, and times when people will respond emotionally. But changes are embraced and lived out when they are linked to a clear vision for mission.

Gregory Ellison uses the term "fear + less dialogues."[7] Ellison acknowledges that there are things that we might fear speaking or thinking or doing. To be "fearless" amid adaptive challenges might not be possible. But we proceed, even with fear. Just less of it.

And this will come with the faith community doing the hard work of asking uncomfortable questions: Who are we, now? Why are we here? What is our purpose? What is God calling us to do and be, now?

As leaders and members in congregations, we might be tempted not to risk adaptive responses out of empathy. That is, we recognize and feel and share the pain of change and are reluctant to ask others to endure that pain.[8] Nevertheless, we are called to say the difficult thing, acknowledge the pain and effort, and continue to follow Jesus adaptively.

Gil Rendle, in *Quietly Courageous*, reminds us that our primary purpose is not to protect and preserve the church.[9] Rather, our call is to faithfully follow Christ. As the *Westminster Catechism* reminds us, the chief end (purpose) of humanity is to "glorify God and enjoy [God] forever."[10] Our *Book of Order* instructs us that the church, as a community of faith, is to entrust itself to God alone, even at the risk of losing its life."[11] In *Necessary Risks*, Teri McDowell Ott writes that we need to ask ourselves whether "our behavior is guided more by our fear...or by the courage we value and seek to live by?"[12]

In our ordination vows, Ruling Elders, Deacons, and Teaching Elders promise that we will "pray for and seek to serve the people with energy, intelligence, imagination and love."[13] That part about imagination is the part that relies on the power of the Holy Spirit: to think imaginatively, to ask the difficult questions, to courageously follow Jesus, into whatever adaptive response God calls us to. And love is the greatest motivator for adaptive change: certainly, love for our Triune God, but also caring and wanting the best for those within the congregation, and the world that the congregation reaches out to with good news.[13]

Questions for discussion:

Do you find it difficult to say difficult things? If so, why? What might help you?

Do you see yourself as an early adopter? A late adopter? A "not at all" adopter (and if so, what are the issues involved?)

How flexible is your congregation? How flexible/willing to change are they? Are you?

What changes, if any, has your Session and congregation made? Are those changes adaptive, or technical, or a bit of both? How were those changes received?

Remember when I asked you to sit, for just one Sunday, in a different space in the sanctuary? How did it feel? What did you learn from that experience? How flexible are you willing to be?

NOTES

1. Charles Cousar, *Galatians*, Interpretation series, (Louisville, KY: John Knox Press, 1982), 35.

2.J. Russell Crabtree, *Owl Sight: Evidence-Based Discernment and the Promise of Organizational Intelligence for Ministry*, 1st ed. (St. Louis, MO: Magi Press, 2012), 112.

3.Darby Kathleen Ray, Incar*nation and Imagination* (Minneapolis, MN: Fortress Press, 2008), 143.

4.Bruce G. Epperly, *Process Theology* (Edinburgh, Scotland: T & T Clark International, 2011), 121.

5.Helen Morris, *Flexible Church: Being the Church in the Contemporary World* (London, UK: SCM Press, 2019).

6. Carmelle Beaugelin, "How do I know whether my church is ready to innovate?," Fa*ith & Leadership*, March 8,2022, accessed November 27, 2023, https://faithandleadership.com/how-do-i-know-whether-my-church-ready-innovate.

7.Gregory C. Ellison II, *Fear+Less Dialogues* (Louisville, KY: Westminster John Knox Press, 2017).

8.Gil Rendle, *Quietly Courageous Leading the Church in a Changing World* (Lanham, MD: Rowman & Littlefield), 2019.

9.Ibid.

9.*PC(U.S.A.) Book of Confessions*, (Louisville, KY: Office of the General Assembly, Presbyterian Church (U.S.A.), 2016), 205.

10.*PC(USA) Book of Order* 2023-2025, (Louisville, KY) F-1.0301, 2.

11.Teri McDowell Ott, *Necessary Risks* (Minneapolis, MN: Fortress Press, 2022), 51.

12.*PC(U.S.A.) Book of Order* 2023-2025 (Louisville, KY) W-4.0404h, 108.

13.Heifetz and Linsky, *Leading Without Easy Answers*, (Cambridge, MA: Harvard University Press, 1994), 210.

Postlude

Reformed, and always being re-formed: faithful transformation

"And remember, I am with you always."
(Matthew 28: 20)

Whew. You made it.

I wonder if you are tired of talking about change.

Tired of living with so much change? Maybe excited by possibilities? Or some mix of the above?

As we have worked our way through this study, I hope you have seen how Scripture, the Word of God, shows us adaptive change.

I found that once I began thinking about adaptive change, it was showing up everywhere.

Sometimes in places I did not expect. And sometimes, many times, it required an adaptive change of me that I did not want. But God is with us in every change.

We have seen these aspects of adaptive change:

That adaptive change is both context driven and context responsive. That adaptive change will require shifts in authority, and will include risk, loss, and failure. That in adaptive change, there will be elements that remain the same, and some that are entirely new. Adaptive change might happen suddenly or occur over a span of time.

And, perhaps most importantly, that an adaptive response is a foundational part of a life of faith, and in and through God's action in adaptive change, we will be changed, too.

As Presbyterians, who have come out of the "Reformed" side of the historic and global church, we often hear the Latin phrase: "Ecclesia reformata, semper reformanda secundum verbum Dei." Often, this is translated as "the church reformed, always reforming, according to the Word of God." That has the feeling of us marching forward and creating change, doesn't it?

But it is more correctly translated as "the church reformed, always to be (or always being) reformed." The Latin is passive.[1] Which means we are being re-formed, whether we like it or not, choose it or resist it.[2] Remember Paul's command to the church in Rome, about "being transformed?" Same idea. Isaiah says the same thing, when he tells us that we are clay, being shaped, meaning changed, by God. (Isaiah 64:8)

Ultimately, blessedly, we are being re-formed by the Spirit of God, according to the Word of God. And we have seen in Scripture how that re-forming, as adaptive response, has been lived out, or rejected, or some combination of all the above. But that doesn't mean it is easy.

You might be ready to be done with all this and want to get back to "life as normal." You might long for "the ways things used to be." But we know that the old ways of being and doing church no longer apply. If nothing else, Covid has taught us this.

But I hope you also have seen, in this Bible Study, that God is still God, and God is still and always faithful. God is still calling us to be in relationship with the Triune God, with each other, and with the world, even in the midst of change.

Let us end as we began, with God's action in Creation.

Revelation 21:1-5

Then I saw a new heaven and a new earth; for the first heaven and the first earth had passed away, and the sea was no more. ² And I saw the holy city, the new Jerusalem, coming down out of heaven from God, prepared as a bride adorned for her husband. ³ And I heard a loud voice from the throne saying,

> *'See, the home[a] of God is among mortals.*
> *He will dwell[b] with them;*
> *they will be his peoples,[c]*
> *and God himself will be with them;[d]*
> *⁴ he will wipe every tear from their eyes.*
> *Death will be no more;*
> *mourning and crying and pain will be no more,*
> *for the first things have passed away.'*

⁵ And the one who was seated on the throne said, 'See, I am making all things new.' Also he said, 'Write this, for these words are trustworthy and true.'

God who created Light, now creates a New Heaven and a New Earth: "See, I am making all things new."

This new creation looks like the old, but it is not the same. There is now not just innocence, but righteousness, not just peace, but reconciliation, and home. [3]

Our hope is always in the Triune God. The Holy One, who begins creation with a word of change, "Light," is still creating, still doing "a new thing," to quote the prophet Isaiah. In the Incarnation and Resurrection of Christ, the new, adaptive thing that God has done and is still doing promises to be with us, even to the close of the age. We have been claimed as a child of God and given the anointing of the Holy Spirit in our baptism. God will change everything, both heaven and earth, even life itself, for death will be wiped away, as will the tears in our eyes.

And so, relying on the Word of God, with flexibility and courage, we follow Jesus, who has promised to be with us in every change. And this life of faithfully following Jesus, since it constantly requires us to shift our habits, loyalties, priorities and beliefs, is an adaptive response.

May God bless us in every change. Amen.

NOTES

1.Michael D. Bush, "The History and Meaning of Semper Reformanda," *The Outlook Magazine*, 48 no. 2, 1998, published January 2020, accessed November 30, 2023, https://www.reformedfellowship.net/thehistory-and-meaning-of-semper-reformanda.md

2.Presbyterian Church (USA), Presbyterian Mission Agency, https://www.presbyterianmission.org/what-we-believe/ecclesia-reformata, accessed October 31, 2023.

3.David Bartlett, "Creation waits with Eager Longing," in *God Who Creates*, ed. William P. Brown and S. Dean McBride (Grand Rapids, MI: W. B. Eerdmans Publishing Co., 2000), 232.

Bibliography

Bauer, Walter et al. *A Greek-English Lexicon of the New Testament*, 2nd edition. Chicago, IL: University of Chicago Press, 1979.

Bartlett, David. "Creation waits with Eager Longing." in *God Who Creates*, ed. William P. Brown and S. Dean McBride. Grand Rapids, MI: W. B. Eerdmans Publishing Co., 2000.

Beaugelin, Carmelle. "How do I know whether my church is ready to innovate?" *Faith & Leadership*, March 8, 2022. Accessed November 27, 2023. https://faithandleadership.com/how-do-i-know-whether-my-church-ready-innovate.

Berlin, Adele and Marc Zvi Brettler, eds. *The Jewish Study Bible*. Oxford University Press, New York, NY: 2004.

Bolsinger, Tod. *Canoeing the Mountains: Christian Leadership in Uncharted Territory*. Expanded edition. Downers Grove, IL: IVP Books, 2018.

Book of Confessions. Louisville, KY: Office of the General Assembly, Presbyterian Church (U.S.A.), 2016.

Book of Order, 2023-2025. Louisville, KY: Office of the General Assembly, Presbyterian Church (U.S.A.).

Brown, Francis et al, *The Brown-Driver-Briggs Hebrew and English Lexicon.* Peabody, MA: Hendrickson Publishers, Inc., 2005.

Brown, William P. *The Seven Pillars of Creation.* New York, NY: Oxford University Press, Inc., 2010.

Bush, Michael D. "The History and Meaning of Semper Reformanda." *The Outlook Magazine*, 48 no. 2, 1998, published January 202. Accessed November 30, 2023. https://www.reformedfellowship.net/thehistory-and-meaning-of-semper-reformanda.md.

Carter, Nick. "Adaptive Leadership: Planning in a Time of Transition" *Theological Education*, Volume 46, 2 (2011).

Chisholm, Thomas. "Great is Thy Faithfulness." Carol Stream, IL: Hope Publishing Company. 1923, 1951.

Cleghorn, John. *Resurrecting Church.* Minneapolis, MN: Fortress Press, 2021.

Cleveland, Christena. *Disunity in Christ: Uncovering the Hidden Forces That Keep Us Apart.* Downers Grove, IL: InterVarsity Press, 2013.

Cousar, Charles B. *The Letters of Paul.* Nashville, TN: Abingdon Press, 1996

Cousar. *Galatians, Interpretation series.* Louisville, KY: John Knox Press, 1982.

Coutts, Peter. *Choosing Change: How to Motivate Churches to Face the Future*. Herndon, VA: The Alban Institute, 2013.

Crabtree, J. Russell. *Owl Sight: Evidence-Based Discernment and the Promise of Organizational Intelligence for Ministry*, 1st ed. St. Louis, MO: Magi Press, 2012.

Dweck, Carol. *Mindset*. New York, NY: Ballentine Books, 2016.

Ellison II, Gregory C. *Fear+Less Dialogues*. Louisville, KY: Westminster John Knox Press, 2017.

Epperly, Bruce G. *Process Theology*. Edinburgh, Scotland: T & T Clark International, 2011.

Farrell, Hunter B. and S. Balajiedlang Khyllep. *Freeing Congregational Mission*. Downer's Grove, IL: InterVarsity Press, 2022..

Fretheim, Terence E. "The Repentance of God," in *What Kind of God? Collected Essays of Terence E. Fretheim*, Ed. Michael Chan and Brent Strawn. University Park, PA: Penn State University Press, 2015.

Hartford Institute for Religious Research, 2020. "Twenty Years of Change: The Faith Communities Today Overview." Accessed November 5, 2023. https://faithcommunitiestoday.org/wp-content/uploads/2021/10/Faith-Communities-Today-2020-Summary-Report.pdf.

Heifetz, Ronald A. and Marty Linsky. *Leading Without Easy Answers*. Cambridge, MA: Harvard University Press, 1994.

Heifetz, Ronald A., Marty Linsky, and Alexander Grashow. *The Practice of Adaptive Leadership: Tools and Tactics for Changing Your Organization and the World*, 1st edition. Boston, Mass: Harvard Business Press, 2009.

Jones, Robert P. *The End of White Christian America*. New York, NY: Simon & Schuster, 2016.

Keller, Catherine. *On the Mystery*. Minneapolis, MN: Fortress Press, 2008.

Kotter, John. "The 8-Step Process for Leading Change," accessed December 5, 2023. https://www.kotterinc.com/8-steps-process-for-leading-change.

Kotter. *The Heart of Change*. Boston, MA: Harvard Business Review Press, 2002.

Kranz, Gene. *Failure Is Not an Option*. New York, NY: Simon & Schuster, 2009.

Kuzawa, Christopher W. et. al., "Metabolic costs and evolutionary implications of human brain development," *Proceedings of the National Academy of Sciences* (111 (36)): 13010-13015, accessed October 31, 2023, https://www.pnas.org/doi/10.1073/pnas.1323099111.

Lamb, David T. "The Immutability of YHWH." *Southern Theological Review*, 2/1 (Summer 2011).

Langley, Sue. "Why do people find it so hard to change when they know it's good for them?" accessed December 5, 2023. https://langleygroup.com.au/why-do-people-find-it-so-hard-to-change-when-they-know-its-good-for-them/.

Levine, Amy-Jill and Marc Zvi Brettler, ed., *The Jewish Annotated New Testament*. London, England: Oxford University Press, 2011.

Lewis, Karoline M. *John*. Minneapolis, MN: Fortress Press, 2014.

Long, Tom. "Go Tell," *Follow Me Adult Reflection Guide*. Louisville, KY: Growing Faith Resources, 2022.

McDowell Ott, Teri. *Necessary Risks*. Minneapolis, MN: Fortress Press, 2022.

Medina, John. *brain rules*. Seattle, WA: Pear Press, 2008.

Mezirow and Associates. *Learning as Transformation*. San Francisco, CA: Jossey-Bass, Inc, 2000.

Morris, Helen. *Flexible Church: Being the Church in the Contemporary World*. London, UK: SCM Press, 2019.

Pelikan, Jaroslav. *The Vindication of Tradition*. New Haven: CT: Yale University Press, 1986.

Peterson, Eugene H. *The Message Remix*. Colorado Springs, CO: Navpres, 2003.

Popova, Maria. "Why the Best Roadmap to an Interesting Life Is the One You Make Up as You Go Along: Daniel Pink's Commencement Address." *the marginalian* (blog), June 25, 2014. Accessed November 30, 2023. https://www.themarginalian.org/2014/06/25/daniel-pink-northwestern-commencement/.

Presbyterian Church, (U.S.A.), Office of the General Assembly. "Comparative Summary of Statistics. Accessed September 22, 2023. https://pcusa.org/site_media/media/uploads/oga/pdf/statistics/2022_stats_comparativesummaries.pdf.

Presbyterian Church (USA), Presbyterian Mission Agency. Accessed October 31, 2023. https://www.presbyterianmission.org/what-we-believe/ecclesia-reformata.

Ray, Darby Kathleen. *Incarnation and Imagination*. Minneapolis, MN: Fortress Press, 2008.

Reid, Robert Stephen. "Becoming a Built to Change Congregation," *Journal of Religious Leadership* 13, no. 1 (Spring 2014): 32. Accessed October 24,2023. http://arljrl.org/wp-content/uploads/2016/02/Reid-Becoming-a-Built-to-Change-Congregation-2014.pdf.

Rendle, Gil. *Quietly Courageous Leading the Church in a Changing World*. Lanham, MD: Rowman & Littlefield, 2019.

Roxburgh, Alan J. and Fred Romanik. *The Missional Leader* San Francisco: Jossey Bass, 2006.

Savage, Adam. *Mythbusters*, Discovery Channel. Accessed March 13, 2020. https://go.discovery.com/tv-shows/mythbusters/.

Skinner, Matthew L. *Intrusive God, Disruptive Gospel*. Grand Rapids, MI: Brazos Press, 2015.

South Presbyterian Church. "History Summary-2," Accessed October 29m 2023. https://southpc.org/wp-content/uploads/2023/08/History-Summary-2.pdf.

Tickle, Phyllis. *The Great Emergence*. Grand Rapids, MI: Baker Books, 2008.

Vaynerchuk, Gary. "Content is King but Context is God." March 21, 2016. Accessed November 5, 2023. https://garyvaynerchuk.com/content-is-king-but-context-is-god.

Withrow, Lisa R. "Change: Exploring Its Implications for Religious Leadership," *Journal of the Academy of Religious Leadership*, 7, no. 2 (Fall 2008): 48. Accessed December 22, 2020, http://arl-jrl.org/wp-content/uploads/2016/02/Withrow-Change-Exploring-its-Implications2008-Fall.pdf

Wright, Gary and Ivy Wigmor. "What does VUCA really mean?" Accessed December 5, 2023, https://www.techtarget.com/whatis/definition/VUCA-volatility-uncertainty-complexity-and-ambiguity.

Yamada, Frank. "Commentary on Numbers 11:4-6, 10-16, 24-29," Working Preacher, September 27, 2009. Accessed October 25, 2023, workingpreacher.org.

www.ingramcontent.com/pod-product-compliance
Lightning Source LLC
Chambersburg PA
CBHW071016120626
46546CB00003B/1117